Wells Coates

Twentieth Century Architects

TWENTIETH CENTURY SOCIETY

C20

ENGLISH HERITAGE

RIBA Publishing

Wells Coates

Twentieth Century Architects

Elizabeth Darling

Published by RIBA Publishing, 15 Bonhill Street,
London EC2P 2EA

ISBN 978 1 85946 437 3

Stock Code 77475

British Library Cataloguing-in-Publication Data

A catalogue record for this book is available from the British Library.
Commissioning Editors: Lucy Harbor and Matthew Thompson
Series Editors: Barnabas Calder, Elain Harwood and Alan Powers
Production: Neil O'Regan
Copy Editor: Ian McDonald
Typeset by Carnegie Book Production
Printed and bound by W.G. Baird, Antrim

RIBA Publishing is part of RIBA Enterprises Ltd.

www.ribaenterprises.com

Front cover photo: Lawn Road Flats © James O. Davies, English Heritage

Back cover photo: Wells Coates, 1947 © Design Council/ University of Brighton Archives

Frontispiece: The cantilevered galleries at Lawn Road Flats

The
Dancers
Shop

Foreword

My interest in the architecture of the Modern Movement kicked in when I was at the Bartlett School of Architecture in the early 1980s. We were asked to design a house in the countryside and I was struggling for inspiration. My tutor, Steven Groak, lent me his copy of *Modern Houses in Britain 1919–1939* by Jeremy Gould. The effect was immediate and I spent the next few years visiting as many as I could. Sometimes I was chased away by angry owners, furious that I should try to photograph their property, but more often than not I was invited in and shown around their wonderful houses. Connell, Ward & Lucas were my particular favourites. They produced an extraordinary range of houses and I liked to imagine the two New Zealanders sitting alongside Colin Lucas having a great time (they probably didn't – private house clients are often not the easiest!). But when it came to apartment buildings, for me there were two clear winners, Lubetkin and Coates. Lubetkin and Tecton's two blocks of Highpoint flats, built a few years apart, remain inspirational and almost tell the story of British Modernism on their own. I met Lubetkin when he was very old and living in his modest house in Clifton; a charming man with whom I spent a very pleasurable few hours listening to him talk about his life.

The opportunity to work on restoring a Coates building, when our practice was approached by the Embassy Court leaseholders, gave me the chance to re-visit his work and take a fresh look at what he was trying to achieve. I knew his three apartment buildings well. While Palace Gate in Kensington had been well looked after, the Lawn Road Flats in Belsize Park had been in an appalling state for many years and Embassy Court looked like it was on the verge of collapse.

As a project, its refurbishment was as much about the people who lived there and loved the building as it was about the architecture. Years of neglect and legal disputes with the freeholder had allowed the building to reach a state where flats sold for well below market rates. What had surely been the south coast's most glamorous building was a very pale shadow of its former self, and many believed it was beyond salvation. Led by the tireless and determined Emma Jinks, the leaseholders won the battle to gain ownership of the freehold and commenced the even bigger challenge of raising the funds to refurbish the building.

In researching the building's history, I tried to get a picture of Wells Coates and what he was trying to achieve. Having read Sherban Cantacuzino's book many years earlier, it was clear to me that he sat firmly in the premier division of British Modernism. Embassy Court didn't get much coverage in the book, so most of our research came

opposite: **View down Western Street, Brighton, to Embassy Court**

from contemporaneous journals. Luckily a series of working details had been published so elements such as the curved glass entrance doors could be authentically replicated.

Coates's daughter wrote a book that made him out as a rather sad figure, frustrated by the lack of success he believed he deserved, but there is no mention of Embassy Court in it. At the event celebrating the refurbishment she told me he was threatened with legal action before the building was even completed, with windows cracking (they were built in to the concrete so any structural movement would damage them) and water ingress. Fiona MacCarthy however, in her introduction to Jack Pritchard's memoirs (*View from a Long Chair*), places him firmly in the centre of London's cultural elite, with the Lawn Road flats as surely one of the most fashionable places to be seen.

In this book Elizabeth Darling digs deeper and gives the most rounded picture to date of this complicated figure. She looks at how his early life in Japan and his missionary parents shaped his thinking. How his training as an engineer, combined with his constant striving for innovation, using the most modern materials made him a true leader in design, not just of housing (though how people live in the modern age was clearly a passion). His position as one of the leading architects of his generation is fully explained – Darling makes it clear that he was the man to work for if you wanted the very best experience at the cutting edge of architecture.

The development of modern architecture in Britain may have lagged behind Corbusier and Mies but by the late 1930s the UK was producing some of Europe's finest work, with a unique blend of European émigrés and those from the colonies working alongside the Brits. Had it not been for the war, Coates and Lubetkin would surely have been the Rogers and Foster of their day. But the conflict saw practices fold and architects going into the armed forces. Darling looks at Coates's work in the RAF where he continued to design – fighter aircraft and later prefabricated housing.

Darling paints a picture of a man who is not an architect. Coates is an engineer, a product designer, an industrial designer, a teacher, an innovator and a visionary thinker. A leading light and very much at heart of the London (and European) architectural scene at the time – a man who died too soon. Had he lived longer perhaps he would, like Goldfinger and Lubetkin, have been re-assessed by the architectural profession, given the recognition he surely deserved. A flawed genius, and a troubled soul perhaps but surely one with much more to give. This book gives a fascinating insight into the work of one of the most interesting characters that British Modernism produced. With housing again high on the architectural and political agenda, it is a timely reminder of the role of the creative thinker and the need for innovation.

Paul Zara

Acknowledgements

The fact that this book has come to fruition owes much to the efforts and assistance of many individuals, institutions and organisations.

Sincere thanks are owed to Laura Cohn, Wells Coates's daughter, and her family, who were extraordinarily generous about the granting of permissions to reproduce images of Coates's work.

I am most grateful for the funding support for the illustrations and related costs awarded by the Marc Fitch Fund, the Society of Architectural Historians of Great Britain, and the John S. Cohen Foundation.

For help with providing illustrations I am indebted to Catherine Moriarty at the Design Archives, University of Brighton and the wonderful team of Sirpa Kutilainen and Barbara Taylor, as well as Monica Brewis, St Peter's House Library, University of Brighton; Avanti Architects; the Overend family, especially Tronn Overend in Melbourne; Conran and Partners and Morley von Sternberg; Ken Crowe at Southend Museum; Julia Dawson at the Canadian Centre for Architecture, Montreal; Bridget Gillies at the University of East Anglia Archives; Katie Hambrook, Subject Librarian, Oxford Brookes University Library; Susanna Heron; and the Regency Society of Brighton and Hove.

For funding support for research costs I thank the Paul Mellon Centre for the Study of British Art, the RIBA Historical Trust, the Scouloudi Foundation, and the University Sabbatical Fund and the Faculty of Humanities and Social Sciences research fund at Oxford Brookes University.

That the book takes the form it has owes a great deal to Alan Powers, to whom special thanks are extended, and to the photography of James O. Davies at English Heritage.

For support which ranged from the intellectual to the familial, or amicable, and which otherwise meant that I kept my sanity during the process of research and writing I am especially grateful to Matthew and Sheila Craske; David Lawrence; Helen Potkin; Sue Robertson; Lesley Whitworth; and my parents, Morag and Anthony Darling, my sister and brother-in-law, Marion and Kenneth Wood, and my nephews Thomas and Harry Wood. My gratitude is also due to John Allan; Molly and the late Douglas Beard; Alex Buchanan; Hilary Gifford; Philip Goad; John Gold; Emma Jinks, Sue Milnthorpe and Paul Roberts at Embassy Court; Lucy Harbor, James Hutchinson, Ian McDonald, Neil O'Regan, and Matthew Thompson at RIBA Publishing; Elain Harwood; Max Lobatto, Paul McLinden and Jason Thomas at Ocean Wave Pilates, Hove; John and Mary McKean; Roger Strauss; Christopher Wilk; and Paul Zara.

This book is for Michael Brown and Jane Taylor, with affection, and with gratitude for a friendship of many years.

Elizabeth Darling, Hove, East Sussex, summer 2012

TWENTIETH CENTURY SOCIETY

C20

Without the Twentieth Century Society an entire chapter of Britain's recent history was to have been lost. It was alert when others slept. It is still crucial!

Simon Jenkins, writer, historian, journalist

The Twentieth Century Society campaigns for the preservation of architecture and design in Britain from 1914 onwards and is a membership organisation which you are warmly invited to join and support.

The architecture of the twentieth century has shaped our world and must be part of our future; it includes bold, controversial, and often experimental buildings that range from the playful Deco of seaside villas to the Brutalist concrete of London's Hayward Gallery. The Twentieth Century Society joined this collaborative series of monographs as part of its campaigning work. We seek to research the work of key architects of our period, to offer an enjoyable and accessible guide for novice and enthusiast, and to use the books to help make the case for why these buildings should be conserved.

Previous volumes in the series have already had a major impact. Our nomination of 'British Brutalism' to the 2012 World Monuments Watch was successful in part due to Alan Clawley's *John Madin* focusing on Birmingham's Central Library as this architect's outstanding work. The recent Oxford Dictionary of National Biography has also followed our lead and included entries on Donald McMorran (of *McMorran & Whitby*) and Gordon Ryder (of *Ryder & Yates*).

We propose buildings for listing, advise on restoration and help to find new uses for buildings threatened with demolition. Join the Twentieth Century Society and not only will you help to protect these modern treasures, you will also gain an unrivalled insight into the groundbreaking architecture and design that helped to shape the century though our magazine, journal and events programme.

For further details and online membership details see *www.c20society.org.uk.*

CATHERINE CROFT

DIRECTOR

opposite: **The staircase at Shipwrights, Essex, 1937**

Introduction

Over the past two decades, a series of early British modernist buildings – including Tecton's structures at London Zoo; Mendelsohn and Chermayeff's De La Warr Pavilion at Bexhill; Max Fry's Miramonte, Kingston Hill; Ernö Goldfinger's 2 Willow Road, Belsize Park; and Wells Coates's three blocks of flats at Hampstead, Brighton and Kensington – have been variously renovated, conserved and otherwise commemorated. The motivation for this work has varied. While a certain degree of modernist fetishism might account for the renovation of a private (or animal) house, the bringing back to life of more publicly oriented schemes, like Coates's flats, suggests that even 80 years on such projects have a relevance and lessons for the modes and mores of twenty-first-century life in programme, in plan, or both.

In some instances the renovation work has occasioned or coincided with new scholarship both on the buildings and on their architects.[1] As a consequence, our knowledge of the diverse forms taken by interwar British Modernism has expanded substantially since the initial wave of historical work on this period which culminated in the Arts Council's 'Thirties' exhibition in 1979.[2] On the other hand, while renovation has brought a new familiarity to the names of British modernist architects, in some instances that is perhaps all it has achieved. This is especially the case for Wells Coates. Despite the fact that in the past decade his two major residential blocks, the Lawn Road Flats, Belsize Park (1934), and Embassy Court, Brighton (1935), have been completely renovated (by Avanti Architects in 2004 and Conran & Partners in 2006, respectively)[3] – and that Gumuchdjian Architects and John McAslan and Partners have worked on schemes for the foyer and flats at Coates's 1939 block at Palace Gate, Kensington – little new attention has been paid to the processes through which Coates created these deft solutions to the problem of modern urban living, or to the other designs that he produced during his career.

The existing literature, which dates chiefly to that first body of interest in the 1970s, comprises a monograph by Sherban Cantacuzino (now out of print) and an exhibition catalogue and a biography-cum-memoir by Coates's daughter Laura Cohn.[4] All of these studies relied heavily on material from his archive (now housed in the Canadian Centre for Architecture, Montreal), but, given their primary concern to provide a documentation of Coates's oeuvre, they offer neither an historical account of his work and life within the broader context of twentieth-century British architecture nor a more general drawing out of his significance, either for his time or for today. It is, then, to that task, and by drawing on a considerable range of new archival sources, that this book attends.

above: **Wells Coates, photographed in his studio flat at Yeoman's Row, London *c.* 1936**

Like many architectural historians, my introduction to Wells Coates was as one of the 'characters' in the story of the introduction of Modernism to Britain, one which emphasised the role of the 'foreigner' and émigré in the transformation of the nation's architectural culture, a process firmly located in the 1930s.[5] A distrust of this trope of importation, and an interest in the clients who commissioned modernist buildings such as the Lawn Road Flats, led me, in my 2007 book, *Re-forming Britain, Narratives of Modernity before Reconstruction*, to offer an alternative to the established story.[6] My argument was, and remains, that Britain's Modern Movement had already emerged by the time the émigrés arrived, and was rooted in a native progressive tradition which caused a demand for the new formal and spatial language we call Modernism.

In the process of researching that book it became apparent to me just how significant a figure Coates was in the development of British architectural Modernism. It was not simply that he produced some of the most intellectually satisfying and rigorous architecture of the interwar decades, with a sophistication of practice which owed much to his immersion in the most progressive circles in London's art world following his arrival in the city in 1922. It lay equally in his constant effort, almost as soon as he began to practise professionally as an architect in 1929, to bring together other like-minded designers and sympathisers to campaign more widely for the cause of a new architecture and its adoption at a larger scale. It seemed to me that the existing work on Coates, whether monographic or general, did not really understand this, despite the fact that, as early as 1958, his obituarist, J. M. Richards, had remarked 'that modern architecture owed more to him than it was customary to acknowledge'.[7]

In this book, I want to go further towards addressing Richards's claim by exploring Coates's work and life and his inter-relationship with Modernists and progressives in other fields, many of whom became his clients or were more generally influential on him.[8] And it is because I want to emphasise Coates's embeddedness within an unfolding progressive tradition that the book is organised thematically rather than purely chronologically. Thus, the first two chapters consider his early life and the influences which shaped what he saw as the task facing 'the young architect today':

> The function of integrating, unifying and synthesizing a multitude of material details, processes and conditions, and of human desires, needs and appetencies, and of giving to the whole a formal aspect of significance ....[9]

Their focus, therefore, is on smaller one-off projects such as his earliest professional commission, a shop for the silk manufacturer Cryséde, completed in 1929, the significant domestic interiors designed for the left-wing MP George Russell Strauss (1932) and the actors Elsa Lanchester and Charles Laughton (1934), his studio flat at Yeoman's Row, London (1935) and the house, Shipwrights, at Leigh-on-Sea, Essex (1937).

Chapter Three takes a rather different approach. It explores the politics of Coates's architecture: his activity as a ceaseless proselytiser for the modernist cause, which culminated in the formation of the MARS (Modern Architectural Research) Group in early 1933 and, interlinked with this, his concern to become involved with projects which could bring his Modernism to a wider audience. It considers, therefore, projects such as the flats at Lawn Road of 1934, whose clients, Jack and Molly Pritchard, saw it as a prototype design to transform urban living, and the reworking and expansion of this scheme at Embassy Court, Brighton (1935); Coates's work for the wireless manufacturer Ekco (1934–52), which saw modernist design find a niche in the most ordinary of homes; as well as projects for the BBC (1932) and the speculative builders E. & L. Berg Ltd, for whom he developed the Sunspan house (1934).

The book concludes with a discussion of his career during the Second World War, when he served in the RAF, and the rather difficult post-war years when, despite the fact that this period saw Modernism establish itself as a social, aesthetic and institutional discourse in Britain, Coates found it hard to sustain a practice. He did continue to design, producing significant work for Ekco and the delightful Telekinema for the Festival of Britain in 1951, but eventually decided to head to his native Canada where he was working on a number of planning schemes before his sudden death, in 1958.

The work and life which this book traces will, I hope, leave in the reader's mind a sense of the innovative and inventive man who created it and a greater understanding of the significance of the transformation of architecture and architectural culture, in which he played no small role, which took place in interwar Britain.

Notes

1 See, *inter alia*, John Allan, *Berthold Lubetkin, Architecture and the Tradition of Social Progress*, London, RIBA Publications, 1992; Alistair Fairley, *De La Warr Pavilion, the Modernist Masterpiece*, London, Merrell, 2006; Alan Powers, *Serge Chermayeff, Designer Architect Teacher*, London, RIBA Publications, 2001.

2 Jennifer Hawkins and Marianne Hollis (eds), *Thirties, British Art and Design before the War*, London, Arts Council of Great Britain, 1979. The *Architectural Review* devoted its November 1979 issue to a consideration of this decade.

3 The Afterword (pp.131–141) discusses the story of these two major renovation projects.

4 See Sherban Cantacuzino, *Wells Coates, A Monograph*, London, Gordon Fraser, 1978; Laura Cohn (ed.), *Wells Coates, Architect and Designer 1895–1958*, Oxford, Oxford Polytechnic Press, 1979, and her more recent *The Door to a Secret Room, a Portrait of Wells Coates*, Aldershot, Scolar Press, 1999.

5 See, for example, Kenneth Frampton, *Modern Architecture, a Critical History*, London, Thames and Hudson, 1987, Part Three, Chapter 1, 'The International Style: theme and variations 1925–65', pp.252–3.

6 Elizabeth Darling, *Re-forming Britain, Narratives of Modernity before Reconstruction*, London, Routledge, 2007.

7 J. M. Richards, 'Wells Coates, 1895–1958', *Architectural Review*, November 1958, pp.357–60.

8 This book forms part of a much larger ongoing project to research and document Coates's work and life.

9 Wells Coates, 'Furniture Today, Furniture Tomorrow – Leaves from a Meta-Technical Notebook', *Architectural Review*, July 1932, p.34.

CRESTA
CRESTA
CRESTA

1 Becoming an Architect

Like several of those who practised as modernist designers in the late 1920s and 1930s, Wells Coates had no formal architectural training. Yet, by the summer of 1928, he had received his first substantial professional commission to design retail stores for the silk manufacturer Cryséde. Within a year, he would be designing a factory, and the first of eight stores, for another silk company, Cresta.

Coates dated his ability 'to practise my profession alone', as he put it, to 1927.[1] The catalyst for this was almost certainly the transformation of his bachelor bedsit at 32 Doughty Street, London, into a marital home in the summer of that year. A palette of aluminium sheet-board and the plainest furniture, with corduroy curtains decorated with a line painted by the artist John Banting, created an interior which was widely praised by friends. They, he reported in a letter of early 1928, 'say at once: you ought to go in for this sort of thing.'[2] A commission for a drawing room followed, and, as he reflected to his correspondent, he now seemed at a crossroads. Should he carry on with the journalism by which he had been supporting himself since 1924, or seize the opportunity signalled by this new commission? His concluding words make his feelings clear:

> It may be that more [commissions] will come, and so, by degrees I may be able to work up a small business. I should like to do this very much. Further: I am a trained engineer, and I believe that house-building is today the business of the engineer plus the painter. Architects are mostly finished – at least in England. In France Le Corbusier and Mallet-Stevens (two engineers) have done wonderful things ... there may be some hope in the decorating business, to say nothing of the new architecture ... If you could only hear some of the ideas I have in this field![3]

This letter, and that first interior, suggest that Coates not only had the ability to conceive and execute a programme of design but in so doing was making use of the most modern of materials. He was also familiar with two leading avant-garde architects of the day. This was something of a turnabout for someone who, prior to the summer of 1927, had displayed little interest in architecture. What, then, led him to have the confidence, and ability, to accept professional commissions, and to create what was, for the England of the late 1920s, a quite remarkable architectural language?

Arguably the most significant precondition and influence on Coates's emergence as an architect, as well as his first steps towards the creation of an architectural language, was his modernity. From the age of 18, Coates found himself immersed in the 'maelstrom of modern life', face to face with Western modernity at its most progressive

opposite: **Cresta Store, 73 New Bond Street, 1932**

and, sometimes, its most extreme.[4] It would not be until the late 1920s that a second, and ultimately equally important, influence became evident in his designs and his thinking, that of Japanese culture. The assimilation of the two allowed Coates to create some of his finest work.

Coates was born in Japan to parents who were missionaries for the Canadian Methodist Church. Harper (1865–1934) and Agnes Coates (1864–1945) were a formidable pair. Both were highly educated – his father became a Professor of Philosophy and Comparative Religion at Aoyama College, Tokyo, while his mother held a Mistress in Liberal Arts degree and had set up a girls' school in Kofu as part of her missionary work – and were ambitious for their six children, all born between 1895 and 1906, especially their eldest, Wells Wintemute. Although little concrete evidence survives from this period, it seems that as a child he was first tutored privately by Japanese teachers who taught him calligraphy and craft skills, and was, perhaps, taught the more usual Western curriculum by his mother. In his early teens, he was sent away to the south of the country to study with a Welsh-born tutor, G. E. L. Gauntlett, who, as well as preparing him for matriculation so that he could enter university, also taught him to type and take shorthand. The practical emphasis of his education was paralleled by an expectation of independence of character: he was taught to cook and take care of a household, to earn his own pocket money and to budget carefully any money that he was given by his parents.[5]

Once Gauntlett's work was done, the decision was taken to move back home so that Coates could complete his education, and his siblings attend school. Thus, accompanied by his father (who returned to Japan the following September), but with the rest of the family following on later, Coates left Japan for good in March 1913 at the age of 17. Embarking on the SS *Cleveland*, he travelled via stops in China, Singapore, India, Egypt, Greece, Italy and London, and arrived in the Canada which gave him his nationality, but in which he had never set foot, in July that year.

The family reunited, they took up residence in Vancouver. According to his sister Lila, the relocation saw Coates's first direct venture into architecture, as he and his mother collaborated on the design of the new family home.[6] Yet this project does not seem to have awakened any further ambition, and in the autumn of 1913 he enrolled at McGill University College (from 1915, the University of British Columbia) to take the six-year combined BA and BSc degree in Engineering.

The choice of subject was a significant one. Engineering, especially the mechanical engineering in which Coates would specialise, was the quintessential practical science of the Industrial Revolution; the engineer, a definitive figure of the modern age. For Coates to commit himself to a career in this field was, therefore, perhaps without his realising it, to place himself in the trajectory of progress and forward thinking. More practically, it would also teach him skills in draughtsmanship and the preparation of working drawings, and establish a lifelong interest in the mechanics of how things work.

Coates would ally himself more directly with the modern in the wake of his enlistment for war service in November 1916. He reached France, via England, in May 1917 where he joined the 68th battery of the Canadian Field Artillery. Coates's main job was the curiously archaic one of looking after the horses which took supplies to the howitzer guns at the front. Given that the First World War was the first conflict to be fully industrialised, such a disjunction between the past and present of warfare cannot have been lost on an engineering student. Indeed, it was likely heightened by the fighter planes which flew over his unit's encampment, the sightings of which pepper his diaries. Identifying himself firmly with the future of warfare, by November 1917 Coates had applied to join the Royal Flying Corps, which, after 1 April 1918, became the Royal Air Force (RAF).

As the aviation historian Martin Francis has noted, 'the R.A.F. adopted a highly self-conscious aura of modernity. Flyers saw themselves as a completely new class of warriors, men whose bravery and skill would be tested by their ability to wage war using the most advanced technology available.'[7] Ten years later Coates would substitute architecture for war, with equally remarkable results. But he would never see active service. The war ended just as he had finished his training, and he returned to Canada in early 1919 to resume his studies.

Coates graduated in 1922 with first-class honours and a scholarship from the British government's Department of Scientific and Industrial Research (DSIR), to undertake doctoral studies at the East London (now Queen Mary) College of the University of London between 1922 and 1924; his subject, the 'Diesel Engine. Heat Flow and Temperate Distribution under various conditions of load, fuel, etc.'.[8] The remit of the DSIR, which had been founded in 1916, was to foster what would now be called research and development in industry, in order to put British manufacturing on an equally modern footing with its main competitors overseas.[9] An important aspect of this process was the funding of research at university level in order to create a generation of trained research scientists. These activities signalled the beginnings in Britain of the technocratic culture of expertise which would so characterise the middle years of the twentieth century, and it once again placed Coates at the heart of a modernising project.

Journalism and Travel

Although Coates seems to have embarked on his studies with great gusto, it is clear that by 1923 he was becoming increasingly disenchanted with the materialist focus of his doctoral research.[10] The acquisition of a part-time job for the mass-circulation newspaper the *Daily Express* gave him the money to indulge fresh interests, while a new friend introduced him to the world of bohemian London and modern culture at its most avant-garde. This was Alfred Borgeaud: six years Coates's junior, and a student of geography. A dynamic figure, with a mistress who was a painter, he was active in the social life of the college. Coates described him as 'the first male friend to come into my life'.[11]

Over the next three years, the pair reinvented themselves as modern intellectuals, beginning with an extensive reading programme which ranged from the latest in modernist literature (Joyce, Huxley, Woolf) to the key texts of eighteenth- and nineteenth-century philosophy (Rousseau, Hegel, Kant). They also dabbled briefly in communism, joining the 1917 Club, a gathering place in Soho for all those interested in spreading the revolution (political and cultural). Among its *habitués* were Lady Ottoline Morrell, H. G. Wells, the brothers Alec and Evelyn Waugh, Aldous Huxley and Elsa Lanchester.

The completion of his doctorate in the summer of 1924 seems only to have confirmed Coates's inclination away from engineering. His work at the *Daily Express* expanded, and he and Borgeaud now spent more and more time in and around Soho and Fitzrovia. Coates felt at home there, and by 1925 had moved to a bedsit in Fitzroy Street where his neighbours were Vanessa Bell and Duncan Grant, and his circle of friends and acquaintances included the painters John Banting, John Armstrong, Paul Nash and Robert Medley; the progressive lawyer A. P. Herbert and his wife Gwen; and the dancers Frederick Ashton, Rupert Doone and Elsa Lanchester.[12] He became a frequent visitor to Lanchester's cabaret club (and home – she slept in a specially built balcony-loft, accessed via a trapdoor), the Cave of Harmony. It was there that he met his future wife, Marion Grove, then a student at the London School of Economics. Such friends introduced Coates to a world in which conventions – of life, of art, of sexuality, of where to live and how – were constantly challenged and reinvented.

Still, architecture was some distance away. Despite a brief stint as secretary in the architecture-planning practice of Adams and Thompson, where he met, and became friends with, the future modernist architect Max Fry, no hidden vocation was uncovered. Three months in Paris in 1925, at the behest of the *Daily Express*, coincided with the Exposition des Arts Décoratifs, at which he might have seen both Le Corbusier's Pavillon de l'Esprit Nouveau and Konstantin Melnikov's Soviet Pavilion, but he seems not to have been aware of them, returning to London to a job as the *Express*'s Scientific Correspondent.[13]

Borgeaud's and Coates's odyssey was brought to a tragic end in September 1926. The previous April they had embarked on a trip to Canada in order to make their way across the Rockies, hitchhiking and earning their keep by odd jobs. The intention was to live, in Coates's words, 'as far as possible through our *senses alone*.'[14] But on one of their journeys Borgeaud was killed falling from a train carriage. Dreadful this experience may have been, but it proved the final stage in the process which led to Coates becoming an architect. He was, in many respects, reborn as he set about re-establishing his life following his return to London, alone, in December 1926. The room was found in Doughty Street, and sufficient income secured from a job as a press officer for an advertising exhibition at Olympia and a commission for a series of articles for the Vancouver newspaper, the *Province*. He also met up with Marion again and this time the couple decided to marry, whence that fateful transformation of the bedsit. The products of engineering, and, we might conjecture, the aluminium and plywood from which the Sopwith Camels of his air-force days were made, provided him with his materials. The sparse interiors of Fitzrovia's bedsits gave him the confidence to reinvent the form his home could take, and his training as an engineer gave him the skills to translate these inspirations into built form. The challenge henceforth was to see if he could find patrons who shared his desire to reinvent architecture.

The Start of a Career

Luck was on his side. During a road trip in the summer of 1928, he and Marion visited a friend's cottage where they met Alec Walker (1889–1964), the director of Cryséde.[15] Founded in 1920, the company manufactured, and sold by mail order and through retail stores, lengths of silk (hand-block printed to Walker's designs) and ready-made silk garments and accessories. The firm had entered a period of expansion in 1925 when Walker invited Tom Heron (1890–1983), a silk blouse manufacturer based in Leeds, to replace him as Cryséde's manager in order that he could focus on the design work. The men had much in common. Both had strong connections with the avant-garde artistic community, from the Leeds Art Club to the Vorticists and the Bloomsbury Group. And both shared a desire to bring artist-designed textiles to a wider market. Under Heron's leadership, the firm grew, moving to new, larger workshops in St Ives, taking on more staff, and updating and increasing the number of its stores. Coates's modernity must have appealed to someone as familiar with modernist art as Walker, and within a few weeks of that meeting he had invited him to work for Cryséde as the designer and supervisor of construction of the company's stores. Coates accepted, and he and Marion moved down to St Ives, setting up home in Norway Studios, Porthmeor Square. By the

above left: **Interior of The Cave of Harmony, by Dorothea St John George, from *London's Latin Quarter* by Kenneth Hare, 1926**
above right: **'Mr and Mrs Wells Coates', 1928–1929, by Patrick Heron, age 8. Pencil drawing on paper.**

autumn of 1928 he was hard at work overseeing the refurbishment of shops at Exeter and Cheltenham, and preparing designs for a new one at Green Street, Cambridge. This opened in the spring of 1929.

Given that this was Coates's first, and a very public, professional commission, the Cambridge branch of Crysede is a surprisingly assured, if slightly unresolved, piece of design. It certainly did a fine job of focusing attention on the firm's products. A plate-glass window, and door, dominated the façade. Behind this, the window display sat confidently. Raised on a platform at plinth level, this was enclosed by three back-boards, almost certainly painted with aluminium paint, from which were draped lengths of silk, and in front and around which were scattered samples of Crysede accessories.[16] The whole was topped by a curved fascia, made from aluminium panels riveted together, with full-height, somewhat spindly, lettering spelling out the company's name.

The boldness of the front was matched by the store inside. Clothing display was kept to the counter wall on the left, and to the wall the customers faced on entry. Here were two glass-fronted display cases in which were hung dresses; above these were placed display blocks on which were arranged – in vignette – individual scarves. The glass

above: **The Crysede store, Cambridge, 1929**

front of the shop counter, like the shop window, contained artfully draped lengths of silk. Behind it, glass-faced cabinets and drawers contained, and displayed, bolts of silks and further samples of clothing. While this simplicity of display would have struck customers, perhaps the most surprising element of the store interior was the wall to the right of the entrance. Apart from a lettered frieze, the wall, in a dark-stained plywood, was left almost entirely bare. Its sole features were a full-length mirror and, in the centre, a fearsome-looking radiator, above which was placed a display shelf for scarves.

Against such simple surfaces, the vivid hues and supple forms of Walker's silks were displayed to striking effect. This was further enhanced by Coates's use of colour. The aluminium of the exterior was brought inside, and all the woodwork, from skirtings to cabinet frames, was coated in metal paint. A darker hue was used for the staining of the right-hand wall, and for the floor and carpeting. At night, when the shop was illuminated, the impression was of a softly glowing box of jewels.

At a time when it was more common for clothes shops to resemble bazaars, and when architects were only just beginning to grapple with the problem of designing for the new phenomenon of the chain store, Coates's design, in its striking simplicity, offered a model to be emulated. Contemporaries certainly thought so. The Cambridge Preservation Society wrote to Crysède in praise of 'the happy treatment' of the store-front, continuing:

> The street is one which has suffered much from mean buildings and vulgar shops; by your care for design, both as a whole and in detail, you have assisted in its redemption, and given something to it on which the eye can rest with pleasure.[17]

Arthur Trystan Edwards, meanwhile, in a discussion of exemplary modern shopfronts, commended it for being 'particularly elegant'.[18]

Such elegance, and modernity, did not come without a struggle. A continual problem for Coates throughout his early career was that many of the furnishings and fittings he envisaged for his designs were unavailable. Only rarely willing to compromise (as can be seen in the bentwood chairs in the Cambridge interior), from necessity Coates soon had to expand his skills to include furniture and product design, producing drawings of the utmost detail in order to convey what he required. A memorandum of November 1928 gives some idea of his frustration:

> Perhaps it would be well to point out what an enormous amount of detail work is required, just to make men understand how to make new things without making mistakes. It is like organising a revolution.[19]

Despite such troubles Coates could rightly feel gratified at the response to his design, but within weeks of the store's opening the Crysède adventure was over. During the summer of 1929, Walker suffered a breakdown and, following his return to the company, began to dismiss many of the staff who had made the firm such a success since 1925. This included Coates, and Heron who, reluctant to let the experience of the past four years go to waste, moved to Welwyn Garden City where he established a new silk business, which he named Cresta.

top: The counter in the Cryséde store
above: Interior of the Cryséde store showing the stark design of the right-hand wall

Commissions for Cresta Silks

Central to this new venture was the opportunity it offered Heron to create a model of modern ethical retailing. A committed Christian socialist, he sought to bring his beliefs to bear on what he called 'the problems of modern industrialism', which, he argued, 'truckle[d] to any demand which is backed by money.' His solution was a business model, which removed all possible opportunities for adding in extra costs in bringing goods to market, and, as at Crysède, emphasised the importance of quality, good design and affordability in products. At Cresta, 'middlemen' were cut out completely, and the company itself controlled every aspect of commerce from manufacturing to retail. In line with this economic model, short leases were taken on stores in, or close by, chic shopping streets so that, in combination with a low-cost fit-out, the company could gain value (and custom) by association, avoiding expensive long leases. Such techniques enabled what Heron called 'the Christian doctrine of the Just Price'.[20]

A Christian theory of goods complemented the 'Just Price'. Goods, Heron argued, were to be valued only:

> when their enjoyment leads to a further realization of God and his purpose for mankind and society. To achieve this they must really be 'goods', things well designed and well executed, and not the rubbish which modern business, without high motive or true sense of values, is ever seeking to thrust in our way.[21]

Given this attitude, it is not surprising that Heron was keen to bring as many of the Crysède team as possible with him to Welwyn: Coates was on board by August 1929, charged with the task of designing Cresta's factory and headquarters in Welwyn and the retail stores which would be constructed in London and the south-east between 1929 and 1936. The result was a series of interiors that made a resounding statement of Heron's ethos, and which represented a significant refinement of the language that Coates had first essayed in Cambridge.

Within the purpose-built shell of a factory unit at Broadwater Road, Welwyn, Coates's particular task was to create a modern commercial space which would allow Heron to operate his business model effectively. His plan functioned as a production line, which took the raw silk from bolt to cutting table, sewing machine and hand finishing, and thence to either the mail-order department (from which made-to-measure garments would be sent to the four corners of the empire; Cresta's 'floaty' silk clothes were ideal for hot climates) or the company's growing chain of retail stores. These departments were placed in a U-shaped space, with continuous circulation arranged around a central hub which contained the offices and a small retail store.

Coates's choice of materials and colours was equally well thought through, showing his concern to create a working environment appropriate for those making and selling 'goods'. The main materials were mostly inexpensive: breeze block or deal for the partitions which demarcated the separate areas of the business, plywood for furniture frames and stainless steel for door handles. More expensive woods were used sparingly,

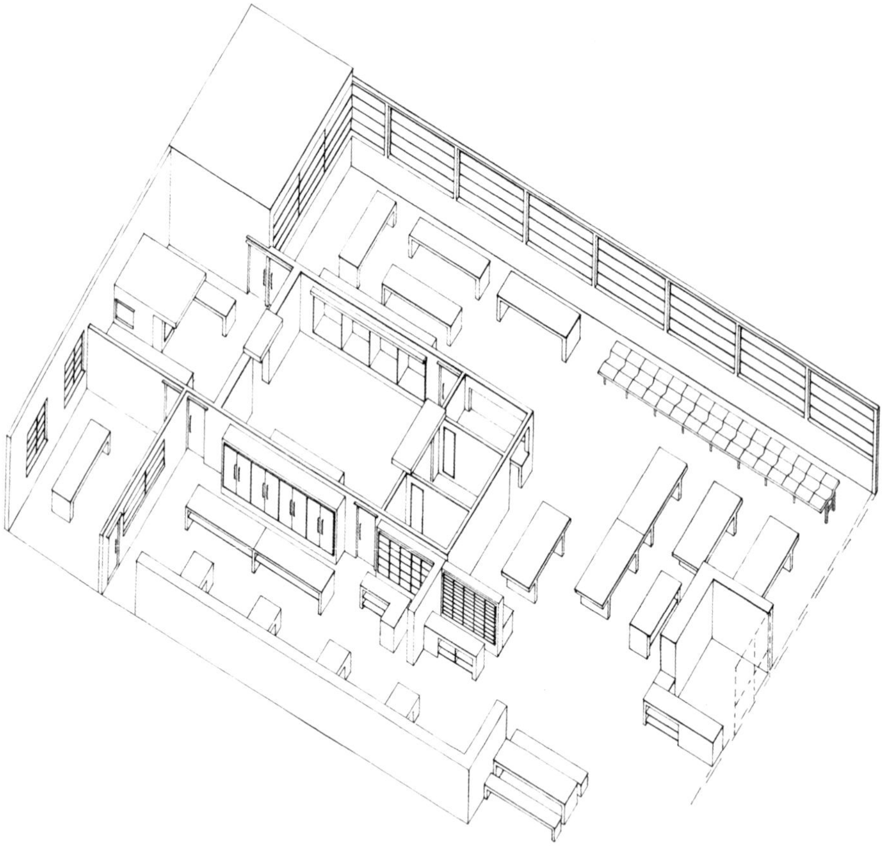

top: Cresta Factory, Welwyn Garden City, 1930: isometric
above: Cresta Factory, interior showing the use of internal panels to subdivide the space

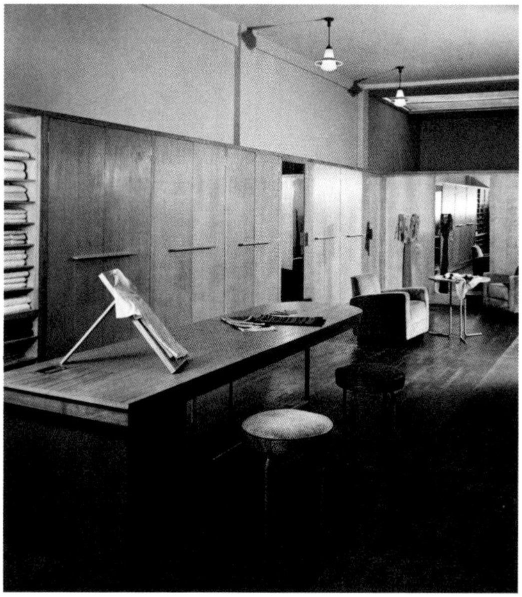

such as oak and alder for cutting table and counter tops. The main structural elements were painted with coats of fine stippled cellulose paint in a pale-flesh tint which would have had a slight sheen. Against this, features such as the cappings to the partitions were painted, again with cellulose, a warm 'drab' colour (a sort of brown-grey hue) and the Saxony carpet in the shop was again this shade of drab.[22] The prevailing tone, the *Welwyn Garden Times* reported, was 'of Rose-Beige'.[23] This dia-chromatic palette represented a simplification of the Crysède interior, in which aluminium, plywood and darker paint and carpets had jostled for attention. But, like the Cambridge store, it provided a carefully contrived setting for the vibrant silks, whether they were stacked in the silk-case fixtures or flowing *en masse* through the rows of sewing machines.

Spatially and formally, this was a deft piece of design – but it was also something much more. In his use of cheap materials, the configuration of plan and the creation of a pleasant working environment, Coates's design offered a physical manifestation of the Cresta ethos of the Just Price and the Christian theory of goods. It also fulfilled two further, and interconnected aims. Heron hoped that his business model would be widely emulated. He also needed to sell his goods in order to demonstrate that the model worked. He therefore needed a distinct brand identity which would promote the company, attracting customers and spreading his vision for an ethical form of modern business. The factory garnered some attention, but Heron knew that it was through its retail stores that he could spread his vision to the wider world. So Coates's next task was

above: **The shop in the Cresta factory**

above: **Standard Lamps designed for the Cresta Store, Westover Road, Bournemouth, 1930**

next page: **Blueprint plan of Cresta Store, Brompton Road**

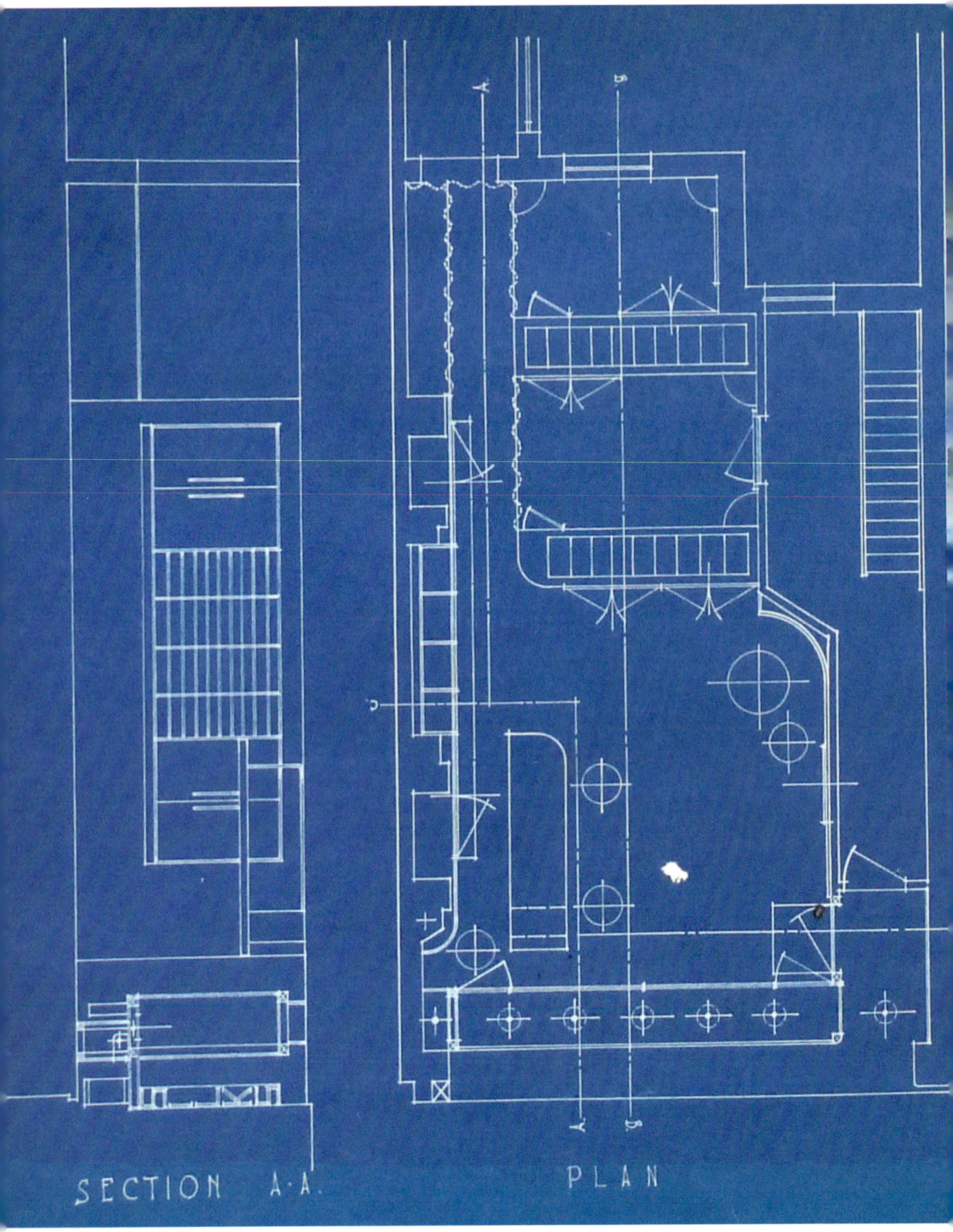
SECTION A·A.
PLAN

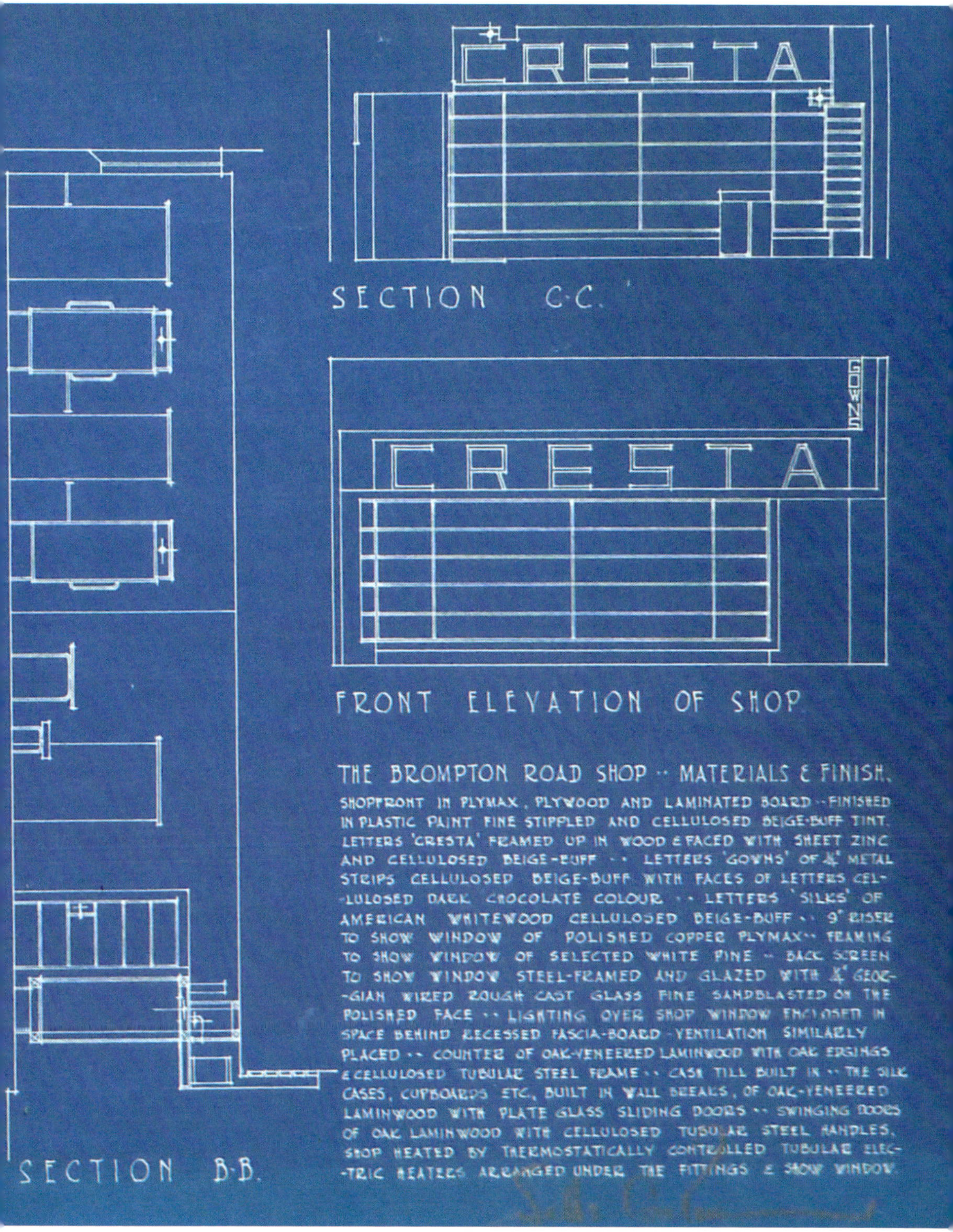
CRESTA
SECTION C.C.
GOWNS
CRESTA
FRONT ELEVATION OF SHOP
SECTION B.B.
THE BROMPTON ROAD SHOP ·· MATERIALS & FINISH.
SHOPFRONT IN PLYMAX, PLYWOOD AND LAMINATED BOARD ·· FINISHED
IN PLASTIC PAINT FINE STIPPLED AND CELLULOSED BEIGE-BUFF TINT.
LETTERS 'CRESTA' FRAMED UP IN WOOD & FACED WITH SHEET ZINC
AND CELLULOSED BEIGE-BUFF ·· LETTERS 'GOWNS' OF ¼" METAL
STRIPS CELLULOSED BEIGE-BUFF WITH FACES OF LETTERS CEL-
-LULOSED DARK CHOCOLATE COLOUR ·· LETTERS 'SILKS' OF
AMERICAN WHITEWOOD CELLULOSED BEIGE-BUFF ·· 9" RISER
TO SHOW WINDOW OF POLISHED COPPER PLYMAX ·· FRAMING
TO SHOW WINDOW OF SELECTED WHITE PINE ·· BACK SCREEN
TO SHOW WINDOW STEEL-FRAMED AND GLAZED WITH ¼" GEOR-
-GIAN WIRED ROUGH CAST GLASS FINE SANDBLASTED ON THE
POLISHED FACE ·· LIGHTING OVER SHOP WINDOW ENCLOSED IN
SPACE BEHIND RECESSED FASCIA-BOARD · VENTILATION SIMILARLY
PLACED ·· COUNTER OF OAK-VENEERED LAMINWOOD WITH OAK EDGINGS
& CELLULOSED TUBULAR STEEL FRAME ·· CASH TILL BUILT IN ·· THE SILK
CASES, CUPBOARDS ETC, BUILT IN WALL BREAKS, OF OAK-VENEERED
LAMINWOOD WITH PLATE GLASS SLIDING DOORS ·· SWINGING DOORS
OF OAK LAMINWOOD WITH CELLULOSED TUBULAR STEEL HANDLES.
SHOP HEATED BY THERMOSTATICALLY CONTROLLED TUBULAR ELEC-
-TRIC HEATERS ARRANGED UNDER THE FITTINGS & SHOW WINDOW.

to adapt the forms of the factory into a brand 'grammar', which would create a distinct corporate image for which Cresta would be widely praised.

Cresta's first two stand-alone retail stores opened in 1930, one at Brompton Road, Knightsbridge, the other at Westover Road, Bournemouth. These were followed by stores at East Street, Brighton; Baker Street and New Bond Street, London; High Street, Bromley; and a second store on the Brompton Road when the original shop was demolished to make way for a block of flats. The ghost of the Cryséde store lingered in Coates's basic blueprint for the shopfronts: a distinctive fascia and large plate-glass display window, backed by some sort of screen behind. At Brompton Road, this was a glazed wooden-framed screen, painted pink; by the time of the Brighton store, the standard convention had become a double layer of floor-to-ceiling-length net curtain. Inside, shop floors were kept clear, but now a standardised form of silk cabinet with sliding doors was built into the wall, and rather than a counter with cabinets beneath, a freestanding table was preferred (the Brompton Road store had the cash register built into the tabletop). Pedestals or stands for the display of dresses were dotted around the stores – as were a standardised design of steel-legged stools and tables, and deep armchairs. Fitting rooms were placed either to the rear of the premises or upstairs, if the store had the space.

top left: **Cresta Store, Brompton Road, London, 1930**
top right: **Cresta Store, East Street, Brighton, 1931**

The colour palette echoed that at Welwyn. Although contemporary reports vary in their terminology for colour shades, it seems that most of the stores had façades coated in a pink/buff semi-gloss cellulose paint, the Cresta letters being picked out in vermilion or beige-buff. The fascias were made variously of laminated wood or metal-faced wood and, sometimes, as at the first Brompton Road store, had glass behind the cut-out letters for effective illumination at night. Inside, the use of oak and birch veneers prevailed for wall panels, woodwork and cabinets, with drab again being favoured for carpets. Some shops had extra features. For the Bournemouth store, for example, Coates designed a striking floor lamp to bring additional light to an interior which was set well back from the street line. But such nuances were minor. The only significant change came after the completion of the Brompton Road and Bournemouth stores with the appointment, in 1930, of Edward McKnight Kauffer to design Cresta's packaging and stationery. Coates's original lettering had been square, and rather clumsy in profile. McKnight Kauffer re-worked this into the distinctive and sensuously curved alphabet which would be used for all Cresta's graphics and was debuted at Brighton in 1931. Finally, in keeping with Cresta's business ethos, none of the shops was built at great expense. The first store at Brompton Road cost just under £1,000, of which £250 was spent on the architecture and architect's fees.[24]

above: **Interior of the Cresta Store, Brighton**

Much to Coates's undoubted delight, the Cresta stores were widely reported in the architectural press: not just the pro-modernist *Architectural Review*, but also *Building*, *Architecture Illustrated* and the US publication *Architectural Record*. Heron would have been pleased that trade journals, such as the *Retail Chemist* and the *Cabinet Maker*, also covered them in detail, emphasising the efficacy of Coates's designs. Although none of the stores has survived, it is not difficult to imagine how impressive they must have been.[25] As at the Cresta factory, Coates had, through his use of materials and space, created a subtle, almost self-effacing, backdrop for the silks, assistants and customers who would inhabit these quiet interiors, and embodied the idea that well-designed things – a shop, a frock or a scarf – should be part of everyday life. The period of sustained work for Cresta, then, had enabled him to develop as an architect and to create an architecture not just of sensibility but also of the intellect.

Creating a Culture for Modernity

Given Coates's background, it should not be surprising that he approached the practice of architecture with the same rigour that he had once applied to his engineering studies and then to his self-fashioning as a modern man. Yet it was something that rather marked him out from his contemporary Modernists in Britain, for Coates was unusual in his desire to theorise his practice and to commit his thoughts to paper; only Berthold Lubetkin and Serge Chermayeff shared this imperative. The nature of this theory was derived, in part, from the reading which he and Borgeaud had undertaken, but, once his vocation became clear, Coates devoted his time to more specifically architectural reading. This allowed him to hone his specialism, but also led him to re-cast some of his earlier interests in the light of this newly acquired architectural knowledge. The result was an unusually clear rationale for his work.

Coates's wide reading of modernist literature, and his friendship with artists, had provided him with lessons in playing with form and convention, and the notion of creating a culture for modernity. His love of the most modern materials – plywood, cellulose paints, aluminium, all of which owed much to technological developments during the First World War – similarly derived from his acute consciousness of living in modern times. Yet these sources do not account entirely for the form of his first designs. Two books, packed in the rucksack carried on that fated Canadian journey, seem to have become of particular importance in this respect: Count Herman Keyserling's *Travel Diary of a Philosopher* and Percy Wyndham Lewis's *The Art of Being Ruled*, both newly published.[26]

Lewis offered Coates the model of the artist-intellectual as the leader of modern society, and the permission to think anew: an influence summarised in Coates's declaration, in 1928, that 'The "Art of being Ruled" stands towards our generation as Matthew Arnold's "Culture and Anarchy" did towards the generation of the seventies.'[27] By 1930, Coates had adopted the persona of a fighter for a modern world of architecture, especially as he sought to organise like-minded fellows in a concerted campaign for the new architecture, as will be seen in Chapter Three.

Keyserling's influence lay equally on Coates's architectural persona and on his architecture. *The Travel Diary* was a two-volume account of the German philosopher's quest for self-discovery on a journey through Sri Lanka, India, Japan, and finally the US. Its appeal to Coates, who had undertaken a virtually identical journey in 1913, must have been irresistible and it presumably offered a model of how to live through the senses alone, which had been the purpose of his Canadian voyage. Re-read in the light of his new vocation, however, the sections on Japan now caused him to look again at his upbringing and knowledge of that country. Hitherto, this had not formed an important part of his identity, but from about 1929–30 Japanese culture became a central point of departure for his theory and practice. One particular passage of the *Diary* proved especially pertinent.

In a discussion of house interiors at Kyoto, an enraptured Keyserling had declared:

> How barbaric is our habit of overloading! How seldom does an object stand in the place which correlation appoints to it! How obtrusive our pictures are! And how rarely is a European aware that a room exists for the man, and not vice versa, that he, and not the curtain or the picture is to be given his best possible setting![28]

Such an observation goes some way to explaining Coates's treatment of space and form at Cryséde and Cresta, and he would use the paragraph, slightly reworded, in many of his theoretical texts of the 1930s. The *Diary* may also have contributed to the adoption of motifs in his architecture which can be linked directly to Japanese sources: *shoji* (sliding screens) or the *tokonoma* (an alcove where a single item of art or an artefact was displayed).[29]

A further aphorism from Keyserling provided another element of Coates's developing persona as an architect. Overwhelmed by the contrast between Japanese interiors and those of bourgeois Europe, the German exclaimed: 'The man whose eyes have been trained in Japan will only rarely want to open them in Europe!'[30] This was paraphrased by Coates into: 'The man whose eyes have been trained in the East will only rarely want to open them in the West', becoming, in an echo of Lewis, a sort of mantra for a primitivism of personality (and, perhaps, design), which allowed him to rethink the conventions and mores of contemporary space.[31]

The influence of Japan, albeit inflected through Western eyes (his own, as well as Keyserling's), was reiterated by Coates's interest in Frank Lloyd Wright. By 1930, Coates was making reference to the American in his writings, noting his insistence on simplicity, that decoration was desecration and that 'good-form is good-sense, put into some effective shape appropriate to some material.'[32] Two articles of 1931 reiterated the relevance of Japan, 'an *inspiration*, not a *precedent*', but also signalled other influences at play on Coates.[33] He references Vitruvius, while his declaration that the plan was the generator of twentieth-century architecture suggests he had been poring over

Le Corbusier's *Vers une Architecture*. This, of course, had much to say about emptying interiors, and only having one good painting, or, as at Cryséde, one good scarf, on the wall.

By 1932, the Fitzrovian and the Japanese, the military and the modern, had, as Coates put it, 'dovetailed', and enabled him to develop a distinctive brand of theory and practice.[34] He was now in a position to fulfil a declaration first made in 1928:

> I believe that the post-war (my) generation is seriously engaged in the task of re-arranging its ideas, both old and new, and honestly laying the foundations for a new synthesis as far-reaching in its importance, its possibilities, as that last great achievement of the Western mind, the Renaissance.[35]

Notes

1 Autobiographical notes for the BBC, 1933, Wells Coates Archive (WCA), Canadian Centre for Architecture, Montreal, Box 4.

2 Coates to Marguerite Broad, letter, September 1927–January 1928, WCA Box 35.

3 ibid. Neither Mallet-Stevens nor Le Corbusier was, in fact, an engineer.

4 Marshall Berman, *All That Is Solid Melts Into Air: the Experience of Modernity*, New York, Verso, 1982, p.16.

5 I draw here from his boyhood diaries, WCA Box 5/E, and the autobiographical notes for the BBC of 1933.

6 Lila Coates to Carol Coates, letter dated 15 February 1972, Carol Coates Archive, University of British Columbia, Vancouver, CCF/11.

7 Martin Francis, *The Flyer, British Culture and the RAF, 1939–1945*, Oxford, Oxford University Press, 2008, p.14.

8 Coates's student record card, 1922–4, Queen Mary University of London Archives (QMUL).

9 On the DSIR, see Organisation for Economic Co-operation and Development (OECD), *Industrial Research Associations in the United Kingdom*, Paris, OECD Publications, 1967.

10 Coates to Marion Grove, letter dated 30 March 1926, WCA Box 35.

11 Coates to Marguerite Broad, letter, September 1927–January 1928, WCA Box 35. See also Borgeaud's student card, QMUL.

12 Robert Medley, *Drawn from the Life. A Memoir*, London, Faber and Faber, 1983, pp.63–5.

13 There is no evidence to support his later claim that he met Le Corbusier at this time.

14 Coates to Marguerite Broad, letter, September 1927–January 1928, WCA Box 35.

15 On Cryséde, see Hazel Berriman, *Cryséde, the unique textile designs of Alec Walker*, Truro, Royal Cornwall Museum, 1993.

16 No specifications for the store survive. The description here draws on surviving photographs and the specifications for a store at Beauchamp Place, London, which was never built, and references to the designs for refurbishment schemes undertaken at this time. See Wells Coates Papers (WCP), CoW/1, RIBA and V&A Archives.

17 A. B. Ramsey to Cryséde, letter of 28 May 1929, WCA Box 7.

18 A. Trystan Edwards, 'Some Modern Shop-fronts', *Architect and Building News*, 8 August 1930, p.188.

19 Coates to Cryséde management, memorandum, 17 November 1928, WCP, CoW/1/1/22(i).

20 Tom Heron, *Christian Vocation in Industry and Marketing*, London, Catholic Literary Association of the Anglo-Catholic Association, 1926, pp.4–6. See also John S. Peart-Binns and Giles Heron, *Rebel and Sage: a biography of Tom Heron 1890–1983*, Bishop Auckland, Pentland Books, 2001.

21 Heron, *Christian Vocation in Industry and Marketing*, p.10.

22 'Cresta', *Architectural Review*, February 1931, pp.45–6.

23 'Real Silks for All', *Welwyn Garden Times*, 30 January 1930, press cutting in John S. Peart-Binns Papers, University of Bradford, 2/2.

24 '"Modern" Shop-Front Design', *Cabinet Maker and Complete House Furnisher*, 3 January 1931, p.17.

25 Following Tom Heron's sale of Cresta in the early 1950s to Debenhams, Coates's shops were dismantled by the Managing Director, Eric Crabtree and replaced by 'pastiche Regency pediments, columns and pilasters' as Patrick Heron wrote in the *Independent*, 22 September 1995.

26 Count Herman Keyserling, *The Travel Diary of a Philosopher*, London, Jonathan Cape Ltd, 1925 (2 vols; translated by J. Holroyd Reece) and Wyndham Lewis, *The Art of Being Ruled*, London, Chatto and Windus, 1926. Coates refers to these two books in his letter to Marguerite Broad, September 1927–January 1928, WCA Box 35.

27 Wells Coates, 'Review of The Art of Being Ruled' (draft) for *The Province* (Vancouver), 16 March 1928, WCA Box 6.

28 Keyserling, *The Travel Diary of a Philosopher*, pp.180–1.

29 For a more detailed outline of Coates's Japonisme, see Anna Basham, 'From Victorian to Modernist: the changing perception of Japanese Architecture encapsulated in Wells Coates' Japonisme', unpublished PhD thesis, University of the Arts, London, 2007.

30 Keyserling, *The Travel Diary of a Philosopher,* pp.180–1.

31 Autobiographical notes for the BBC, 1933.

32 Wells Coates, notes for 'Sketch Plan for a New Aesthetic', 1930, WCA Box 6.

33 Wells Coates, 'Inspiration from Japan' and 'Materials for Architecture', *Architects' Journal*, 4 November 1931, p.586 and pp.588–9, respectively.

34 Autobiographical notes for the BBC, 1933.

35 Wells Coates, 'Books and Persons', draft article for the *Province* (Vancouver), February 1928, WCA Box 6.

above: **Crysede silks swatch book**

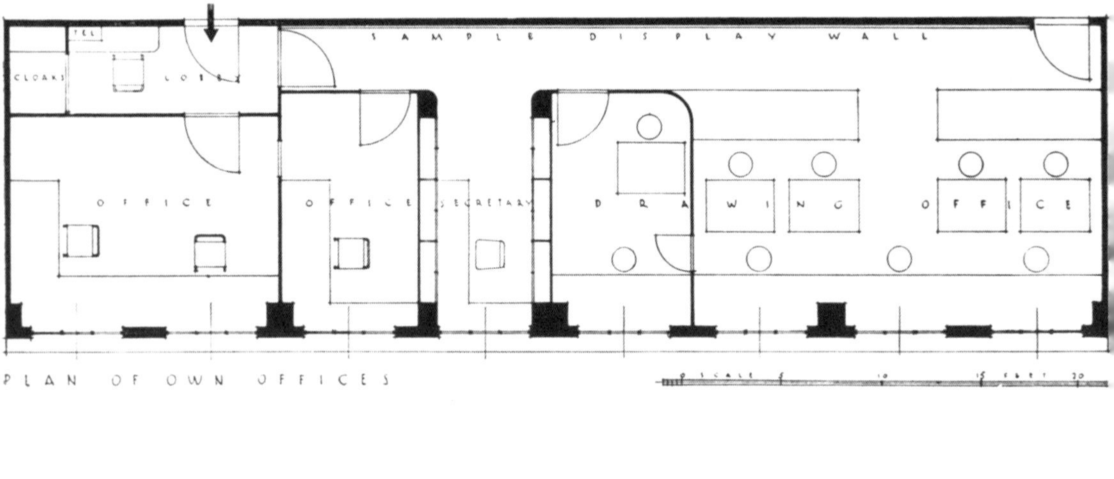

PLAN OF OWN OFFICES

2 A New Synthesis

As a convert to the cause of architecture generally, and modernist architecture in particular, Coates pursued a number of strategies to show how design could play its part in the creation of a new Renaissance in Britain. Many of these were political in nature, and he cultivated alliances and formed interest groups with fellow designers and like-minded reformers in order to promote architectural Modernism to a wider public. At the same time, Coates's own designs served to promote the cause: his distinctive language of architecture at once met the needs of the programme and also served as experiments in the process of working out solutions – in style and method – to the problems facing contemporary Britain.

Central to this process was the patronage of clients, such as Walker and Heron, who were in full sympathy with his ideals. With few exceptions, these men and women were progressives, usually in both their personal and professional lives, coming from fields which ranged from theatre to psychology, from commerce to politics. All were seeking, in one way or another, to reshape British society and culture, and most were linked to the bohemian Fitzrovia of the mid-1920s.

Coates and his clients had self-consciously constructed themselves as modern individuals, keen to shake off the suffocating values and traditions which lingered over post-war British society. This process extended into their homes, and they looked to Coates to help them create environments which would provide a better setting for their lives as a modern couple, a bachelor about town, or a modern family. The lack of appropriate dwellings for such progressive types was, Coates wrote, one of the main obstacles to the achievement of a new society, and he made it one of his primary tasks as an architect to resolve what he described as: 'this problem of *the kind of place* a man and a woman and a family should live in, this problem of the *theatre* of ordinary daily life, the theatre of modern living'.[1] Coates's solution was a distinctive architecture, conceived as a set of tools to facilitate the performance of daily life. This included sequences of interconnected, frequently adaptable, spaces, usually divided by sliding screens (in the manner of Japanese *shoji*), the maximum use of material technologies and equipment, and a colour palette which rarely ventured from cream, drab, green, brown and the odd touch of pink/red/vermilion. This lexicon would be nuanced according to the specific needs of each client, but it had the virtue of retaining sufficient similarity across commissions to brand them as Wells Coates designs, rather than those of one of his contemporaries and competitors.

opposite: **Photographic portrait of Coates with the plan of his office at Elizabeth Street, London, featured in the catalogue of the Unit One group, 1934**

1 Kensington Palace Gardens

Coates's first significant essay in what he later called 'modern dwellings for modern needs' resulted from a commission of early 1932, when the soon-to-be-married politician George Russell Strauss (1901–93) had asked him to redesign the interiors of his London mansion.[2] He and his fiancée Patricia O'Flynn (1907/08–87) were both *habitués* of the clubs and galleries of bohemian London. O'Flynn had been an artist's model, while Strauss was a collector of modern art and an early patron of John Armstrong, who produced a number of artworks for the new interiors (including two for the lavatories), so it was probably through him that Strauss and Coates met.

Patricia was an advocate for birth control and nursery education, and with her husband later commissioned Coates to design a nursery school in Holland Park. George was both an MP and a member of the London County Council, and sat to the far left of the Labour Party. A close ally of Stafford Cripps and Aneurin Bevan, he was heavily involved in their campaign to move Labour away from its moderate parliamentary line and make it a socialist party proper. Very much a backroom boy of politics, one of the requirements for his new home was therefore that it should provide the salon spaces necessary for supporters and 'co-conspirators' of the Labour Left to meet and mingle. At the same time, the house also needed to provide a setting appropriate for the marital, and later family, life of the new couple, and mark their incumbency and identity on a dwelling which had been inherited from Strauss's parents.

One Kensington Palace Gardens (1KPG) was a substantial Italianate mansion of the 1840s, overlooking the Bayswater Road and adjacent to Hyde Park. Strauss's father, a multi-millionaire metal merchant, had bought the house in the 1890s and had it refurbished for his marriage in 1893. The astonishing late-Victorian interior he commissioned was still intact when Strauss inherited it. Its dismantling served as a metaphor for the break from the familial past represented by marriage, but equally the rejection of late-Victorian and Edwardian values which was so central to the Strausses' and Coates's generation. Its replacement, in turn, was a visual metaphor of the modern world they sought to create.

In some respects, however, the house remained tied to tradition. The ground floor, at least, as the site for a political salon, had to be designed as a quasi-public space. Coates, therefore, arranged this floor, and the basement beneath it, as a 'machine for entertaining', and treated the ground floor interiors as a sequence of increasingly grand spaces (signalling his understanding of the classical doctrine of decorum, no doubt derived from his reading of Vitruvius). On entering the house, visitors came first to an entrance lobby and then passed through a series of sliding screen doors to an entrance-cum-staircase hall and finally the waiting hall. Both the lobby and entrance hall had Induroleum floors (a new material made of compacted wood and asbestos powder) and cellulosed walls; the latter had a dramatic set piece (a *tokonoma*) of a copper-plated tubular-steel table with pink rough-cast glass top and

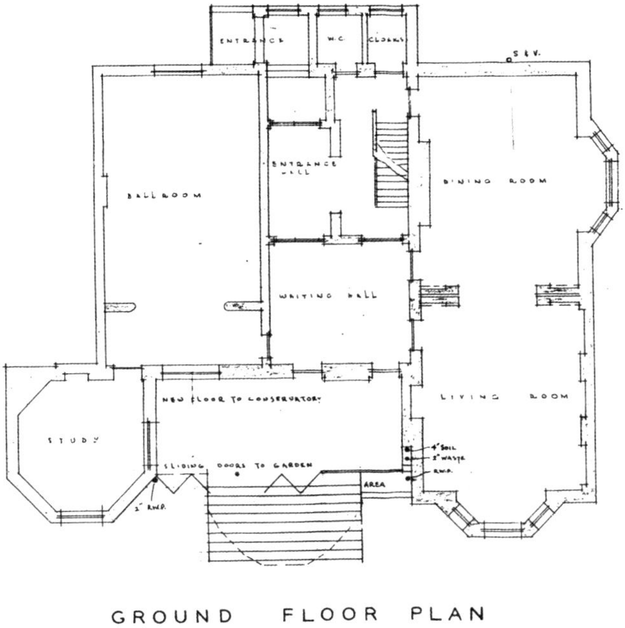

top: **Entrance Hall at 1, Kensington Palace Gardens**
above: **Plan of the ground floor of 1 Kensington Palace Gardens. 1932**

circular mirror (1.7 metres [5½ feet] in diameter) set off by red-lacquered screen doors. The waiting hall, befitting its role as the interface between the house's main spaces, was carpeted, had more furniture – a telephone table, clock, divan and another set piece: a redesigned fireplace with back, surround and hearth all of copper Plymax – and a frieze executed by John Armstrong.

To the right of the waiting hall was a ballroom, replacing what had been the house's main private space, a drawing room. Its interior was muted, a treatment in keeping with a space which would be 'decorated' by the people within. Its most dramatic features were another frieze by Armstrong and the large copper-Plymax fire which was set into the wall. Leading off the ballroom was Strauss's study, easily, and discreetly, accessible should the need for more intimate discussion arise.

above left: **The waiting hall at 1 Kensington Palace Gardens: before its redesign in 1893**
above right: **The waiting hall at 1 Kensington Palace Gardens: after its redesign and with frieze by John Armstrong**

To the left of the waiting hall were the living room and dining room: spaces for small social gatherings such as a cocktail or dinner party, but also for the daily life of the Strausses. The very naming of the living room is noteworthy, signifying not a space apart, as the (with)drawing room had been, but a space which accommodated the various modes of living across day and night, a redesignation in keeping with Coates's notion of the house as a theatre for modern living. Crucial here was the use of screens rather than doors to divide space. These allowed a flexibility and variability of use, so that by day, screened off from the dining room, the room served as a living space with large easy chairs and a sofa, and a writing desk for Patricia. The opacity of the screens allowed some privacy, but their mobility and translucency suggested a preference for an openness far removed from the dusty, dark recesses of the previous Victorian interiors.

above left: **The drawing room at 1 Kensington Palace Gardens: before redesign**
above: **The ballroom at 1 Kensington Palace Gardens: after redesign**

In the evening, the furniture could be rearranged, and the *shoji* screens closed across the bay windows, to create the atmosphere for a cocktail or bridge party, the table for which, like all the other furniture and equipment in the house, was designed to Coates's specifications. At this point, the interior's main feature, the enormous wall fitting, came into its own. Veneered in Australian burr walnut, and built in across the width of the wall, it contained all a host and hostess could need: a wireless and speaker in the centre was flanked by a cocktail cabinet to the left and a gramophone player and record storage to the right. This mechanical 'orchestra' also provided music to the ballroom through extension speakers. Coates even added acoustic side bands to the ceilings to assist sound transmission throughout the interior.

The dining room was similarly well equipped, and reflected Coates's love of technological showmanship. From the redesigned basement kitchen, a service lift rose up through a carpet-covered opening in the dining-room floor to the amazement

above left: **Study/dining room at 1 Kensington Palace Gardens: before redesign**
above right: **Living room at 1 Kensington Palace Gardens: after redesign**

and entertainment of guests. Its contents were then transferred for service to a new sideboard above which was fixed a decorative panel, again by Armstrong. The most notable feature of this space, however, was the dining table: a three-metre (ten-foot) long piece of burr-walnut-veneered Laminwood carried on steel legs encased in pale-green rough-cast glass, each illuminated at the top. The high-backed chairs, Coates declared, gave 'formal significance to the scale of the room' and, perhaps, owed not a little to the influence of Frank Lloyd Wright's prairie house interiors.[3] Family recollections suggest that the colour scheme was based on varying tones of drab and cream, similar to the Cresta shop interiors.[4] Light was diffused through carefully placed, concealed built-in electric fittings, and by the *shoji* screens of 'pale self-colour Shantung silk' between the spaces, and across the windows.[5] The effect of the screens being opened as the party progressed from living room to dining room can be imagined.

above left: **Study/dining room at 1 Kensington Palace Gardens: before redesign**
above right: **Dining room at 1 Kensington Palace Gardens: after redesign**

top: Bedroom at 1 Kensington Palace Gardens: before redesign
above: Master bedroom at 1 Kensington Palace Gardens: after redesign

The sophisticated tone of the public spaces on the ground floor contrasted with Coates's treatment of the suite of rooms on the first. Here the setting was to be for a modern companionate marriage, and comprised a boudoir, dressing room, bedroom with antechamber, and a bathroom. The effect was sensual, with fitted wardrobes made of Laminwood veneered with grey-stained sycamore, a mirrored wall, fitted carpet and silky bedcovers in the master bedroom. There was even a touch of Hollywood in Patricia Strauss's dressing table, which had double-backed mirrors of different tints that rotated so she could see herself in varying lights, while the bathroom was refaced in black glass.

The modernity of these interiors was most evident in their stark lack of decoration, but in keeping with the social and architectural Modernism of both clients and architect, for whom the harnessing of technology to everyday life was an intrinsic part of the project

above: **Dressing table in the master bedroom at 1 Kensington Palace Gardens**

to modernise Britain, this aspect extended to the very materials and technologies of the new interiors. As in all Coates's later architecture, there was scarcely a traditional material to be found in the design; even the carpeting was fitted rather than the more usual fashion of rugs over parquet. The woods used for panelling and furniture were either Laminwood or plywood, the artificiality of these manufactured woods often enhanced by the staining of the veneers with which they were faced. Much of the occasional furniture was tubular-steel framed, while the floors, when not carpeted, were made of Induroleum. Wall surfaces were either faced with plywood panels or coated with the new cellulose paints. The inclusion of technologies such as the service lift and the living-room wall fitting, though hardly likely to feature in the typical suburban semi, were indicative of the idea that technology could and should be mastered. Moreover, much of the house's ability to function as a modern environment was predicated on its complete rewiring (at this point, the National Grid was six years into its construction and significant swathes of the country remained unconnected to this definitively modern source of power). This process allowed the provision of extensive networks of lighting, always carefully choreographed according to purpose, and power points, such as the one that brought electricity to the synchronic clock in the waiting hall.

A final aspect of the modernity of these interiors was their appearance in the contemporary media. As a former journalist Coates was acutely aware of the value of publicity, and he had already seen how much press attention the interiors for Cryséde and Cresta had attracted. Coverage of the project would provide valuable advertising for his skills as an architect, and for the new architecture as a whole. So, in what would turn out to be a series of collaborations with the *Architectural Review*, Coates succeeded in having its July 1932 supplement on 'Decoration and Craftsmanship' devoted to 'before and after' pictures of the house and a lengthy article by him, 'Furniture Today, Furniture Tomorrow – Leaves from a Meta-Technical Notebook'.[6] Although rather convoluted, the text offers an elaboration of Coates's positing of the house as theatre. He wrote:

> The dwelling-scene of tomorrow will contain as part of its structure nearly all that today is carried about for the purpose of 'furnishing' one house after another ... Thus furniture ... will take its place in the logic of construction, becoming an integral part of architecture. For the rest, clothing, bedding, crockery, utensils, books, pictures and sculpture will have the select value of a personal environment; will be, in fact, the only 'furniture' (personal belongings) in use.[7]

The accompanying images (many of which are reproduced here) were similarly powerful, and quickly became a visual shorthand for change in many discussions of the new architecture and design. Within a year they featured in the pamphlet published to coincide with the BBC's series of talks, 'Design in Modern Life', while in his 1937 book, *Interior Decorating*, the designer Duncan Miller would observe of the before and after images of the master bedroom, 'No wonder that such houses have been pulled down or completely replanned the moment their owners died. Nobody conscious of existing traditions would be mad enough to try, even if he were fool enough to want, to carry on such a tradition.'[8]

34 Gordon Square and the Old Vic

A similar rejection of the past may be seen in Coates's next significant domestic commission, for the actors Elsa Lanchester (1902–86) and Charles Laughton (1899–1962). Coates had known Lanchester since the mid-1920s, but it was not until 1933 that she and Laughton (who married in February 1929) set up a permanent home in London, when the latter was engaged for that year's season at the Old Vic theatre. In anticipation of this, and while Laughton was away filming, Lanchester looked for a suitable dwelling, finally settling on the three upper floors of a house at 34 Gordon Square, a development of the early 1820s by Thomas Cubitt, and a stone's throw away from the homes of assorted members of the Bloomsbury Group. The flat housed a full-blown Victorian interior, which Lanchester described as being 'so full of ... furniture that it looked ready to suffocate anybody; one could hardly move without knocking over ivory elephants or knick-knacks.'[9] As at 1KPG, the period clutter was stripped out and, in its stead, Coates created 'the open liveable place' into which this rather curious couple moved in the summer of 1934.[10]

Perhaps even if it had not been designed for actors, 34 Gordon Square would have epitomised Coates's notion of the home as theatre, furnished only with what the individual could carry. The Lanchester–Laughton union was a *mariage blanc*. He was gay, she was not, and their partnership was increasingly devoted to the end of progressing Laughton's career. Lanchester's previous homes had been a series of small

top right: **Elsa Lanchester and Charles Laughton in the sitting room at 34 Gordon Square**

bedsits furnished with a mattress, a couple of chairs and a few pictures, and, later, the domestic perch in the loft of the Cave of Harmony (see Chapter One).[11] As the son of Scarborough hoteliers, Laughton had grown up living in hotel rooms, the most impermanent form of accommodation. It is, then, hard to see the new flat as having been anything but a formalised setting for the continuation of such ad hoc lives and the public 'performance' of their partnership; indeed, when an extensive article was published on the interior in 1938, its title was, tellingly, 'Background for Talent'.[12]

Across the three floors of the house, Coates created a sitting and dining room, a maid's room, a cook's room (they employed Virginia Woolf's former cook, Nellie Boxall), a bedroom each and a spare room-cum-office. As at 1KPG, in response to the demand for more casual living, the opening between the two main public spaces could be masked by three sets of screens, acting as sliding doors, each allowing for a different effect according to the occasion. The centre element comprised panelled *shoji* screens. Either side of these were plywood screens painted by John Armstrong with different scenes: facing the sitting room was one of oleander trees and horses, while, facing the dining room, a jungle scene featured monkeys, zebras and giraffes. The sitting room was dominated by a bookcase fitting which ran the length of the space; this contained

above: **The dining room at 34 Gordon Square, 1933, showing John Armstrong's jungle scene on one of the three sets of sliding doors**

a built-in lighting trough along its top, which illuminated the flower arrangements that, together with one of Laughton's collection of paintings (he owned a Renoir, a Rousseau and an Utrillo), constituted the main 'furniture' of the space according to Coates's definition.

Upstairs, the space became private and contained the couple's bedrooms. These were separate and, although they had an interconnecting door, there was an understandable contrast with the harmonious design and matching twin beds of George and Patricia Russell Strauss.[13] Each was designed to suit the tastes and needs of its inhabitant. Continuing the theme of confounding domestic expectations, Laughton's featured curtains made from roller-towel fabric (Lanchester's were made of shirt material, and there was a matching bedcover). A synthetic-sunshine light hung above Laughton's bed, and there was a cabinet for his china and pottery collection. Lanchester had a writing desk, and a wall of built-in wardrobes.

The reform of domestic conventions permeated the social life as well as the design of their new home. Boxall recalled the couple's refusal to treat the servants as inferior beings: 'And they would talk to you – you know, as if you could read and write. And they had discussions with you.' Guests cleared their own plates away to a service shelf in

above: **The sitting room at 34 Gordon Square**

the hall, as Boxall and the maid were not expected to wait at table. She remarked, 'I've seen Marlene Dietrich carry out dirty plates.'[14] The simplicity of the whole flat surprised some of the guests at the couple's frequent parties, as Lanchester explained: 'the flat was rather unfurnished, but not quite as unfinished as most people thought.'[15] But this emptiness made it all the more a set, in which what furniture there was became props. Thus Bernard Leach, whose ceramics Laughton collected, recalled, 'how well they foiled each other, he and his wife; how delightfully and spontaneously they proceeded to act and play around the sofa in that room!'[16]

In its performed nature, the interior had much in common with a second commission from Laughton. As part of his negotiations for the season at the Old Vic, Laughton secured the theatre's patronage of Coates to provide a permanent set for the 1933 season, and of John Armstrong to design costumes for several productions. These commissions formed part of a bigger plan, instigated by the new Director of the Vic, Tyrone Guthrie, to modernise its productions, moving its Shakespeare repertoire away from the prevailing tradition of pastoral settings to one based on the Elizabethan model. The project as a whole was funded by the Pilgrim Trust, on the basis that the Old Vic's work represented a move towards the creation of a national theatre.[17]

above: Two views of the sitting room showing John Armstrong's second set of sliding screens, and the translucent shoji screens running between the two sets of painted panels

top: **Elsa Lanchester's bedroom**
above: **Charles Laughton's bedroom, with painting by Maurice Utrillo**

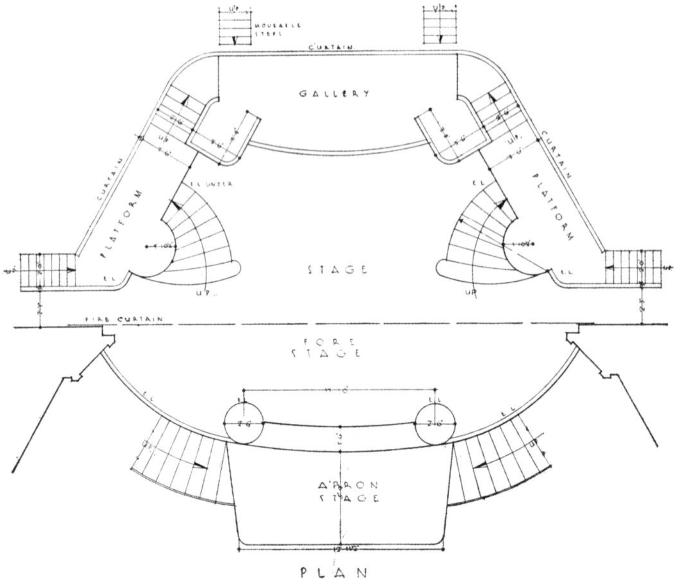

top: **Permanent set for the Old Vic Theatre's 1933 season**
above: **Plan of the Old Vic permanent set**

Comprising two flights of stairs joined by a giant-column flanked gallery, this plywood and canvas leviathan failed to blend into the background and was widely criticised. The *Evening Standard*'s critic called it 'an architectural contraption of nouveau art solidity involving flights of steps ... which would have suited a new hotel at Le Touquet.'[18] Guthrie would recall that he eventually worked out the best way to light Coates's set, but that he had been too inexperienced a client for the architect.[19] His was a signally insightful observation. Coates's enthusiasm for his vocation meant that he

above: **Permanent set for the Old Vic Theatre's 1933 Season. Charles Laughton and Flora Robson are performing**

was a dedicated architect, but one prone to flights of fancy as new ideas took hold. As Cyril Sweett, quantity surveyor to most interwar Modernists, remarked, 'Wells is a chap ... who would be improving the arrangements of the foundation bolts in an Eiffel Tower long after it should have been topped out.'[20] Coates's best work came when he operated under some sort of constraint, as at the Strausses', when a certain economy of funds seems to have stayed his hand, or, as with Laughton, his client's eminence caused him to be 'malleable and docile'.[21] His less successful work, as will become apparent in Chapter Three, was the result of clients who were either more interested in money-making, or did not exert sufficient control over him.

Coates as his own Client: Offices

The commissions at Kensington and Gordon Square, and also those for Cresta, established the architectural vocabulary on which much of Coates's subsequent oeuvre would be based – scaled up or down according to circumstance, as his commission for the flat of man-about-town and trainee psychoanalyst, Pryns Hopkins, shows.[22] But what happened when Coates was his own client? As his very first design for the Doughty Street bedsit suggests, the environments he created for himself served at once to make a declaration of personal (or, as in this instance, marital) identity and also as locations in which to work through ideas about his architectural language. Thus, the office he designed for himself at 33 Bedford Place in 1931 can be understood as a studio in the equal senses of workshop and test bed for schemes of design and equipment to be used in subsequent commissions. Similarly, the new office into which he moved in the latter part of 1932 was designed to be as modern in form and organisation as were the architects it housed and the designs that would be produced there.

The office was at 15 Coastal Chambers, Elizabeth Street, and formed part of the development of the new Victoria Coach Station, designed by Wallis Gilbert and Partners. They became Coates's neighbours; a machine-tool maker was another. Laid out along the window frontage of the block, the premises was divided by a series of glass screens into offices for Coates and his new partner, David Pleydell-Bouverie,[23] a space for the secretary and then the drawing office. As an indication of Coates's love of materials, the entire length of the main office wall was taken up with a rack of sample materials which could be slotted out for reference. Such systematisation was mirrored in the meticulous office routine that Coates instigated, under which every discussion, meeting, phone call and drawing was recorded on specially designed memo sheets, with each project given an identifying acronym (such as 1KPG or 34GS). At the end of each day these were collated by the secretary on to a large record sheet, which then formed the basis for charging customers: a modern business practice then rarely found among architects. It is perhaps not surprising that in his entry for the *Unit One* book in 1934

top: **Wells Coates's office at 33 Bedford Place, London, 1931**
above: **Flat at 2 Devonshire Street, London, for Pryns Hopkins, 1933**

(see Chapter Three), for which contributors had been asked to provide a self-portrait and a picture of their hands, Coates substituted a plan of his office for the latter, for it was through this mechanism that his architecture was produced.

Coates as his own Client: 18 Yeoman's Row

The most complete insight into Coates as both man and designer is, however, to be found in the flat he designed for himself at 18 Yeoman's Row, Knightsbridge, following his separation from his wife in 1935. It was designed over a period of about a year, and he moved in during February 1936, living and later working there (with the exception of the war years) until he moved permanently to Canada in 1956. The site was the top floor of a terraced house in a street just off the Brompton Road, one of eight purpose-built in 1898–9 to include artists' studios at the top, not far from the first Cresta store and its successor and within walking distance of the Elizabeth Street office.[24] It provided a basic shell of space, approximately nine metres (30 feet) deep, five metres (16 feet) wide and four metres (12 feet) high, the whole lit by a large mansard window. Coates's programme was a highly personal one, reflecting his new status as a single man-about-town (his resemblance to the film star Ronald Coleman contributing to his reputation

above: **The interior of Coates's studio flat at Yeoman's Row, London, before work began, 1935**

as something of a ladies' man). He required the largest possible living and studio space, since the new flat was to be a place primarily devoted to entertaining and for designing, and two bedrooms (one for him and one for his daughter or a guest), a kitchen, bathroom and storage space.

The determinant of the design was the four-metre floor-to-ceiling height. This, as he acknowledged in an article on the scheme for the *Architectural Review*, did not allow two floor levels.[25] It was, however, sufficiently high to allow him to devote the largest amount of space, in plan and section, to the part which would be used most. Thus, he created one main living area whose height extended the full four metres, and which occupied about two thirds of the overall floor plan. Into the remaining third of the space were slotted two storeys, in which were placed, at ground-floor level either side of the entrance lobby, the bathroom (with fitted wardrobe) and the kitchen. The living space itself was zoned for dining and for cocktail-party entertainment by the use of the built-in wall fitment and freestanding dining table and chairs. For more intimate or relaxed entertainment, and reflecting his dislike of big sofas and easy chairs for his own use, Coates created what he called a 'hearth-scene *à la japonais*, penned off by a shaped fitting which is a bookcase on one side and a back-rest for cushions on the other'. Its height, he wrote, was such that one's glass, book or cigarettes were easily at hand, while the radiant electric fireplace was arranged so that heat could be directed according to need. Music was provided by a gramophone and wireless, which were built into the service tower that formed part of the back 'wall' of the hearth-scene. The final feature was a tubular-steel ladder which led, surely rather precariously after an evening's entertainment, up to Coates's sleeping area.

Coates was at the heart of this dwelling scene, whether playing the host in the main space or holding court to disciples in the hearth-scene. Patrick Gwynne, who joined

above: **View from the 'hearth-scene' into the main space at Yeoman's Row**

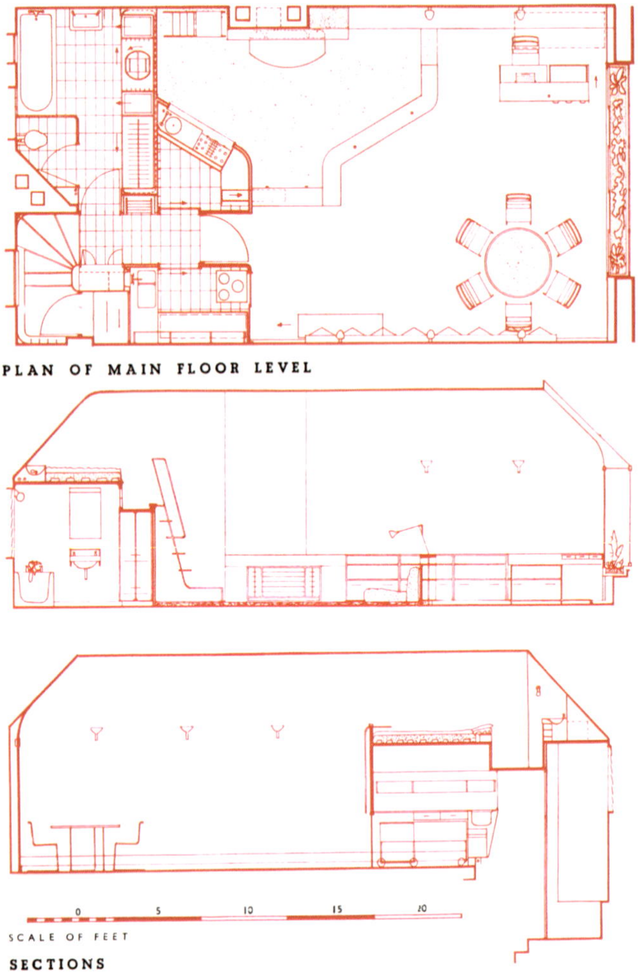

his practice in 1935, recalled the excellence of Coates's parties and his cooking. More of a challenge, however, were the arrangements of the hearth-scene to the average guest: 'Everyone except Wells, who could happily squat eastern style, [was] very uncomfortable on the padded seating area but not daring to say so.'[26]

If Gwynne's recollections hint at the way Yeoman's Row signified the public face of Coates to the world as a sophisticated modern man, the fact that it was he alone who could squat happily in the hearth-scene suggests another aspect of his character: his uncompromising commitment to an idea when unfettered by the demand of the client (something also signalled by his substitution of the armchairs and sofa seen at 1KPG and Gordon Square for that uncomfortable perch; with the exception of four dining

above: **Plan and sections of the studio flat at Yeoman's Row**

top: **The 'hearth-scene' and main living space at Yeoman's Row**
above: **The perspex encased wireless at Yeoman's Row. Its 'backdrop' is a study for the mural at Embassy Court**

chairs and the typing chair, there was nowhere else to sit). Moreover, a discussion of the detail of the design says much about Coates's conceptualisation of space, and therefore his design process. It signals the extent to which Coates's architecture was indebted to his training as a mechanical engineer and derived from that profession's fundamental concern with how objects, and their components, might be best connected in order to serve a particular function.

The hearth-scene, for example, while forming a discrete space within the flat as a whole, was in fact intimately related to the spaces which surrounded it through the central service tower to which it abutted and the fitment which marked its footprint. The lower level of the tower, with sufficient headroom to stand in, contained a small servery, with refrigerator, and a sliding tray through to the drinks cupboard which formed part of the hearth's 'wall'. This was designed with a double aspect, and sliding

above: **Coates photographed at his typing desk at Yeoman's Row, showing the vivarium between the layers of double glazing**

shelves so that glasses and drinks could be reached easily whether in the hearth-scene or the main living room. The fitment itself, which was formed of reinforced concrete covered in light-grey rubber sheeting, with plywood shelves painted Eton blue, contained fixed points into which Anglepoise lamps (invented in 1932) could be fitted, their mechanical arms focusing light according to the user's needs.

On the other side of the room, the ladder to the spare cabin was designed to glide up the wall surface in order to allow a sliding door below to be opened and thereby release a serving trolley into the room from the kitchen, where it was stored beneath the worktable. Meanwhile, Coates's typing desk (he rarely handwrote anything), which is shown in plan in the zone opposite the dining table, could be slotted into the wall bookcase, its top thus forming an additional buffet tabletop for parties.

It is striking how kinetic this interior must have been when in use, requiring the active participation of the inhabitant to make things work. Coates's description of the way he had designed his typing desk is revealing in this respect: 'I like to type on a table which is delicately balanced with a foot-rest bringing the knees tight under it, so that with the spring steel chair, the whole ensemble allows one to "ride" the machine.'[27] This almost cyborg-ian conception of design reflected not just the influence of his training but also his growing interest in the design of yachts, a preoccupation which had begun in the early 1930s, equally evident in the design of the stairs to the bedrooms and their naming as 'sleeping cabins'. Such a knitting together of elements to form a working whole, changeable according to need, represented the apogee of Coates's reimagining of the dwelling as a form of mechanised equipment. This was epitomised in his design for the radio in the hearth-scene, its case made from perspex so that the inner workings were illuminated.

Coates's main assistant on Yeoman's Row was Patrick Gwynne (1913–2003), one of the young architects he had taken on as the practice enjoyed its most fruitful run of commissions between 1932 and late 1938. By 1935, those who had worked, or were working, in his office included the Australian Acheson Best Overend (1907–77), Rodney Thomas (1906–96), Edric Neel (1914–52), John Wheeler (1915–45) and Denys Lasdun (1914–2001). Lasdun had been keen to join Coates, considering him and Tecton to be the best modernist practices to work for.[28] He and Wheeler had trained at the increasingly progressive Architectural Association school in London, while Neel had been at Cambridge and Thomas at the Bartlett school, University College, London where he had preferred the company of artists to that of architects. Gwynne was converted to Modernism as a schoolboy at Harrow and had trained as an articled pupil. This assembly of young talent encouraged Coates to experiment more in the way he designed, as may be seen in the desire to exploit the full potentialities of the section at Yeoman's Row. It may also have been connected to Coates's increasing number of commissions for whole buildings, which had begun with the blocks of flats at Lawn Road and culminated in the designs for the practice's two main private-house commissions, Shipwrights, completed 1937, and The Homewood, completed in 1938.

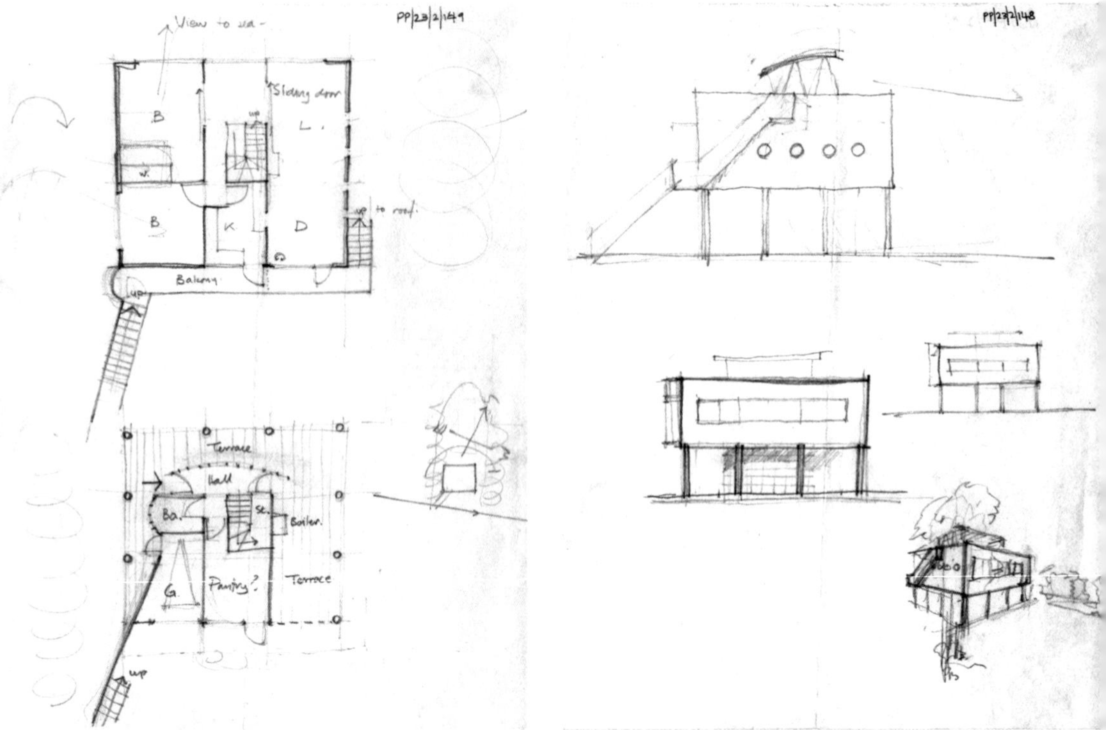

Shipwrights

Shipwrights was designed as a weekend house for John Wyborn, the Chief Engineer of Ekco, the wireless manufacturer for whom Coates produced some of his most delightful works of product design (discussed in Chapter Three) as well as a new factory at Southend in 1936. The men appear to have enjoyed a good working relationship, following Wyborn's approach to Coates in early 1934 to work for the company.[29] The site was in Leigh-on-Sea, on open wooded land sloping steeply to the south overlooking the Thames Estuary: a view which would prove central to the conceptualisation of the design. The logical response, which Coates took, was to raise the house on *pilotis*, and to place the living room and main bedroom on the south side of the dwelling in order to take maximum advantage of the riverscape from the windows. The use of this device, as well as the ribbon window along the south elevation, has obvious echoes of Le Corbusier's Villa Savoye of 1929, as commentators have observed.[30] But this does not necessarily imply thoughtless copying. Coates was certainly not alone in his use of *pilotis* when faced with the same programmatic demand.[31]

At approximately eight by eight metres (25 feet by 25) the house was not a large one, but it offered Coates another opportunity for deft planning. Having entered behind

above and right: **Sketch designs by Coates for Shipwrights, *c.* 1937**

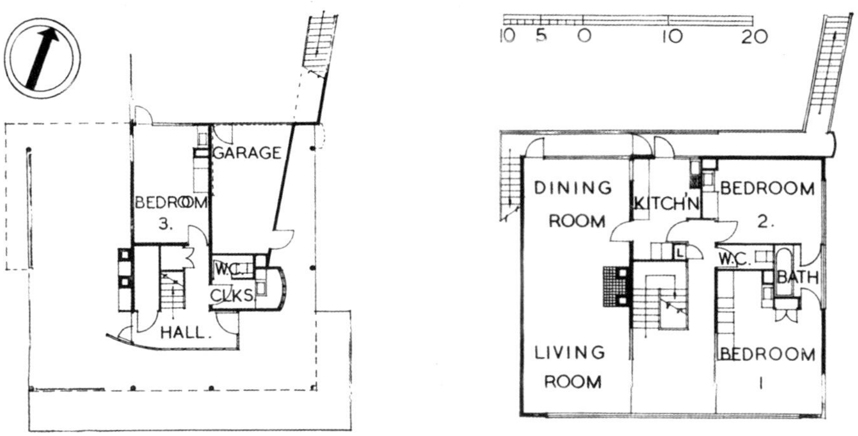

top: **Entrance side of Shipwrights**
above: **Plans of ground and first floors**

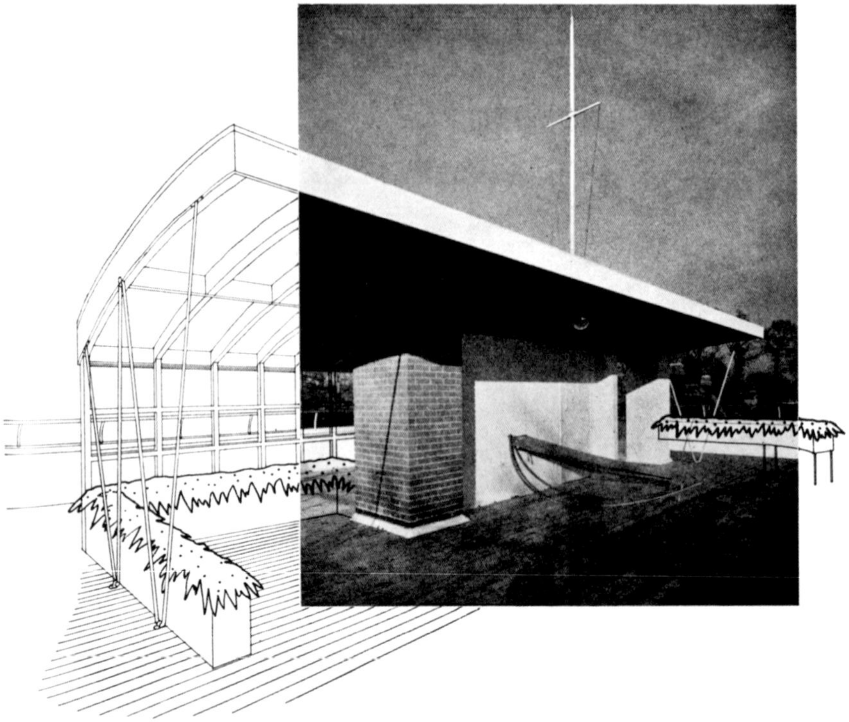

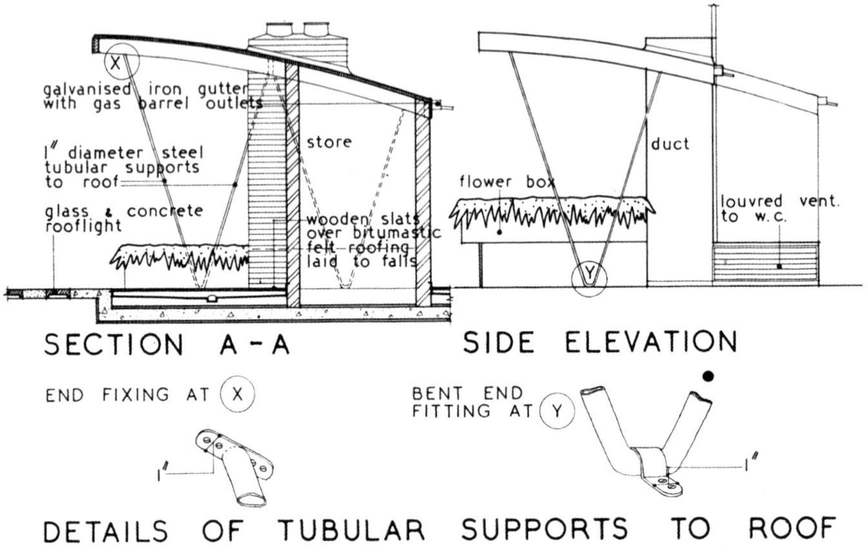

above: **Photomontage and sections of the Shipwrights roof shelter**
previous pages: **The garden front of Shipwrights**

the trellised screen which formed the entrance wall, one ascended directly into what was, in effect, a *piano nobile*, with the living-dining room filling the western third of this level, and the main bedroom, to the east, separated from the broad landing at the head of the stairs by sliding doors. The kitchen, second bedroom and bathroom fitted into the remaining north-eastern quadrant. With the sliding screens pulled back, the two sides of this upper level made one continuous L-shaped space, with the *fenêtre en longueur* of the south elevation framing a continuous panorama. Beneath the *pilotis* to the western side, the ground-level accommodation (third bedroom, cloakroom and garage) was enclosed by a brick wall – Coates's first use of the material and deliberately non-loadbearing, unlike the concrete structure. The wall contained a fireplace, making a sheltered outdoor room. An external stair ascended to a balcony on the north side serving the kitchen, and carried on to the rooftop, where a sun terrace commanded the view from beneath an aerofoil-curved timber canopy.

Coates stuck to his usual muted colour palette for the house. The plaster render of the façade was tinted a light blue, while inside the dominant hue was cream, with oak and cork flooring (as well as some carpeting), and some strongly patterned textiles for curtains and bedcovers. The by now standard built-in fitments in the living-cum-dining room were veneered in beech.[32]

above: **The dining area at Shipwrights**

The Homewood

The design of Shipwrights clearly relates to The Homewood, at Esher, Surrey, which followed it. Around 1937, Coates had developed a system of associateships in the office: a form of not-quite-partnership which allowed assistants to bring their own projects into the office and work on them as principals, while also continuing as assistants on the practice's other projects.[33] The scheme brought work and money into the office at a time when most of the firm's major projects were nearing completion and new commissions becoming scarce. On this basis Gwynne brought a proposal for a substantial new house for his father, Commander A. L. Gwynne, replacing a large but dilapidated Victorian villa, standing close to the increasingly busy Portsmouth Road on four hectares (10 acres) of woodland. Its replacement, on higher ground away from the road would be, as the architects later wrote, 'a country house: a house, that is to say, with country setting and seclusion: but one with remarkably rapid access to London.'[34]

According to Gwynne, Coates suggested that a large version of the Sunspan house type (discussed in Chapter Three) would be the solution, but he was outvoted by the Commander and his son. Gwynne recalled later that he had been working on this scheme before joining Coates's office, where he was the assistant on Shipwrights. And it was from these plans, with some contributions from fellow assistant, Denys Lasdun, who suggested the oval pool on the garden terrace, that The Homewood developed,

top left: Built-in fitment in the Living-Dining Area at Shipwrights
top right: View through to the kitchen from the dining area at Shipwrights
opposite: Photomontage for publication of the living-dining room at The Homewood

ALG

HOUSE AT ESHER

LIVING & DINING ROOM

ARCHITECTS PATRICK GWYNNE & WELLS COATES

THE LIVING ROOM is designed to combine a background for entertaining with the informality of an all-purpose room.

IN SUMMER the main scene is set against the large windows.

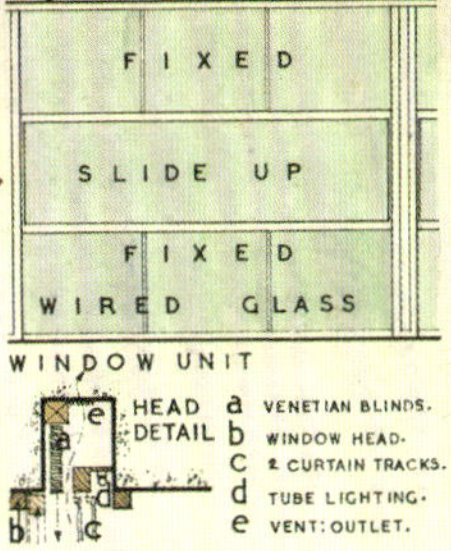

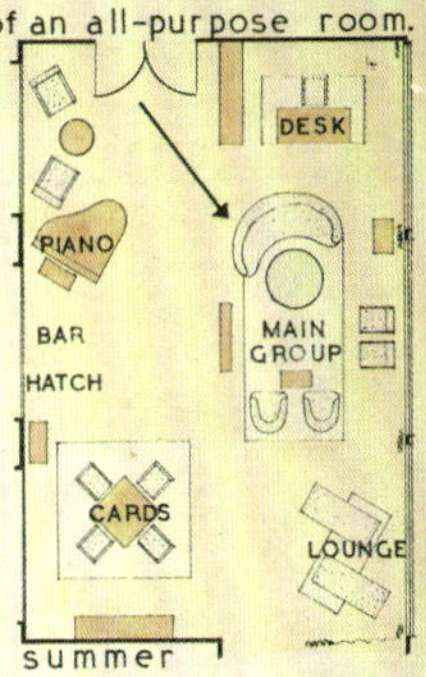

AT NIGHT the room is lighted from the head of the windows and the interior of the display cabinets in the wall.

IN WINTER the main scene is set against the fireplace wall.

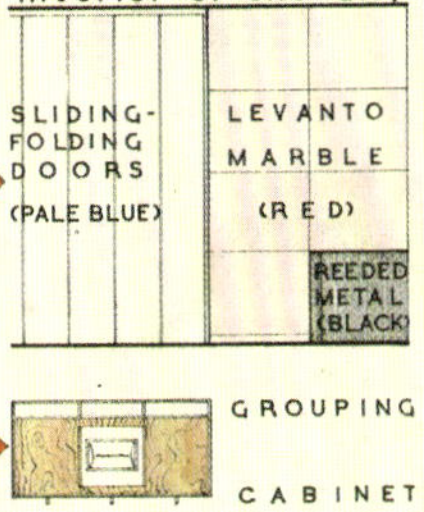

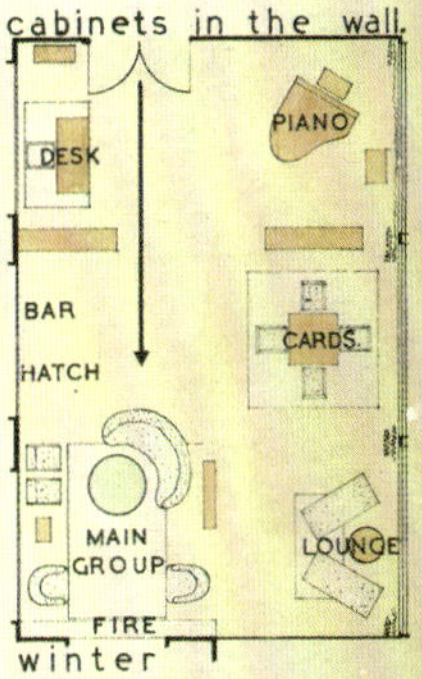

THE FITTED WALL is a formalised design of decorative and utility compartments; display, hatch, radio, etc:

MOVEABLE CABINETS are used to define groups of furniture.

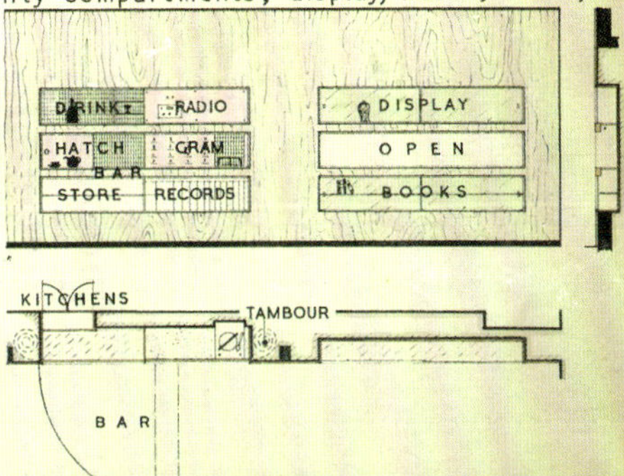

THE DINING ROOM is designed as a continuation of the living room, separable by means of a folding partition.

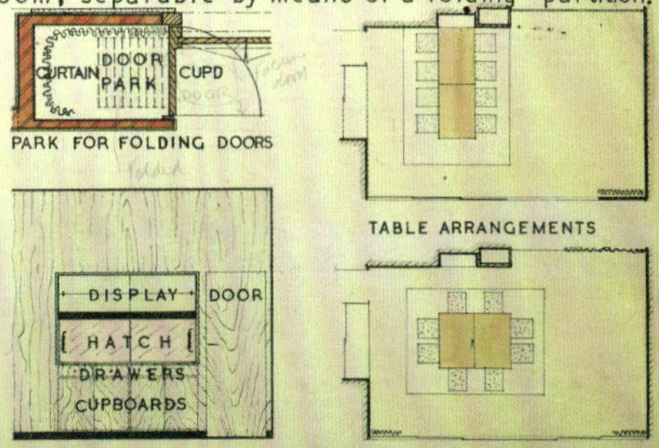

an acknowledgement of suggestions and technical advice from Coates. Some ambiguity over the balance of attribution remains.[35]

Although The Homewood is much larger, in site and scope, than Shipwrights, the designs have much in common. Principal floors were arranged at first-floor level, and the central staircase of the Essex house became the bridge between the two wings of the dwelling (one primarily for bedrooms, the other containing the main living room and dining room with services at both first and ground level). The exterior elevations have echoes of Shipwrights, as does the use of a brick wall of the same red-brown hue at ground-floor level. The planning of the interiors owed much to Coates in the merged space of the living and dining room, the connected spaces of the bedroom and boudoir units (as at 1KPG), and the extensive deployment of built-in fitments to serve these spaces. While Coates would have approved of the reinforced-concrete structure of the house, Gwynne favoured expensive and traditional materials, such as maple, Brazilian rosewood and marble veneer, rather than the synthetic products of recent date preferred by Coates. The overall effect of the house, then, is that of a master's design vocabulary translated into a more decorative, and perhaps decadent, language by his pupil.

The fact that a stint in Coates's office was widely sought after by students gives some idea of his appeal to an architectural audience, as well as a sense of the longer-term

above: **The garden side of The Homewood, Esher, 1938 (enamel panels by Stefan Knapp added in 1960s)**

impact his approach would have on the next generation of card-carrying Modernists. But if the new architecture were to really gain ascendancy, as he believed it should, Coates needed to address the issue of demand, as well as that of supply, and bring his Modernism to a much wider audience than he had hitherto enjoyed.

Notes

1 Coates to Jack Pritchard, letter of 13 July 1930, Jack Pritchard Archive (JPA), University of East Anglia, PP/23/1/26.

2 Wells Coates and Geoffrey Boumphrey, 'Modern Dwellings for Modern Needs', *Listener*, 24 May 1933, pp.819–22.

3 Wells Coates, 'Furniture Today, Furniture Tomorrow – Leaves from a Meta-Technical Notebook', *Architectural Review*, July 1932, p.37.

4 Interviews with Roger Strauss (June 2009) and Hilary Gifford (July 2009).

5 Coates, 'Furniture Today, Furniture Tomorrow', p.36.

6 The before images of the house were taken in 1893, and re-used for this article.

7 ibid, p.34.

8 Duncan Miller, *Interior Decorating*, London, The Studio Ltd, 1937, p.70.

9 Elsa Lanchester, *Charles Laughton and I*, London, Faber and Faber, 1938, p.135.

10 ibid, p .9.

11 ibid, p.85.

12 Joan Woollcombe, 'Background for Talent', *Woman's Journal*, October 1938, pp.52–6.

13 On the politics of the marital bed and bedroom, see Hilary Hinds, 'Together and Apart: Twin Beds, Domestic Hygiene and Modern Marriage, 1890–1945', *Journal of Design History*, Vol 23, no. 3, 2010, pp.275–304.

14 Nellie Boxall, interviewed in George Ewart Evans, *From Mouths of Men*, London, Faber and Faber, 1976, pp.80–4.

15 Lanchester, *Charles Laughton and I*, p.200.

16 Bernard Leach, *Beyond East and West. Memoirs, Portraits and Essays*, London, Faber and Faber, 1978, p.124.

17 Memorandum of 29 March 1933, Pilgrim Trust archive, No. 1814/The Old Vic, London Metropolitan Archives.

18 *Evening Standard*, press cutting for 19 September 1933, WCA Box 16.

19 Tyrone Guthrie, *A Life in the Theatre*, London, Reader's Union/Hamish Hamilton, 1961, p.109.

20 Cyril Sweett, quoted by Randal Bell in a letter (undated) to Laura Cohn cited in *The Door to a Secret Room, a Portrait of Wells Coates*, Aldershot, Scolar Press, 1999, p.217.

21 Tom Laughton, *Pavilions by the Sea. The Memoirs of a Hotel-Keeper*, London, Chatto and Windus, p.82. It was because he did not feel he could exert the same authority that Laughton (Charles's brother) decided not to commission Coates to work on the redesign of a hotel in Scarborough.

22 'The English Living Room To-day', *Design for Today*, May 1933, pp.12–13.

23 David Pleydell-Bouverie (1911–94) had made a name for himself as an interior designer before joining Coates in 1932, presumably bringing some finance into the new partnership. He had left the office by 1934, going on to design, most famously, Ramsgate Airport. He left England permanently in 1937 to settle in California.

24 See Survey of London, vol. XLI, *Southern Kensington: Brompton*, London, Athlone Press, 1983, pp.125–6.

25 Wells Coates, 'Planning in Section', *Architectural Review*, August 1937, p.55. All quotations are taken from this article until signalled otherwise.

26 'Wells Coates', Recollections by Patrick Gwynne, April 1979 in Denys Lasdun Papers, RIBA and V&A Archives, LaD/1/2.

27 Coates, 'Planning in Section', p.58.

28 Interview with Patrick Gwynne and Denys Lasdun by Alan Powers, National Sound Archive, British Library, F6778, 31 July 2008. There were also technical/drawing assistants whose names are unknown.

29 According to M. I. Lipman, *Memoirs of a Socialist Businessman*, London, Lipman Trust, 1980, p.70.

30 For example, Sherban Cantacuzino, *Wells Coates, A Monograph*, London, Gordon Fraser, 1978, p.85.

31 See, for example, Marcel Breuer's Sea Lane House, Angmering (1936–7).

32 The house was reported in 'House at Hadleigh, Essex', *Architects' Journal*, 29 June 1939, pp.1119–22 and 6 July 1939, pp.17–18, and Alan Hastings, *Week-end Houses, Cottages and Bungalows*, London, The Architectural Press, 1939, pp.30–1.

33 The hairdressing shop in Canterbury with Edric Meel of 1937 is another example.

34 'House at Esher' Surrey, Patrick Gwynne and Wells Coates, Architects, *Architectural Review*, September 1939, p.103.

35 The National Trust, to which Patrick Gwynne gave the house in the 1990s, attributes it solely to him.

3 Marketing Modernism

In seeking to extend the market for Modernism, Coates and like-minded architects faced a challenge. The fact was that however much he and they might believe that their work offered a blueprint for the reshaping of Britain, throughout the 1930s their client base remained small and almost exclusively confined to wealthy and more than usually progressive individuals or organisations. A problem, too, as a distinctly modernist agenda emerged in the last years of the 1920s, was the lack of any coherent group identity which might function to persuade decision makers, or at least those with influence upon them, of the benefits to be gained from the patronage of modernist architects. If Modernism were to move beyond a restricted client base and regional focus in the south-east of England, then its advocates needed to develop a more strategic approach to their work.

Coates played a leading role in the process of moving Modernism from the margins to the mainstream, seeking, as this chapter explores, to work on projects through which he might extend the idea of the home as a mechanised environment beyond a circle of elite individuals. Alongside this he developed a particular identity for the modernist architect, emphasising their role as the engineer, literally and metaphorically, of a new society. By presenting the architect's task as one of problem solving and prototyping solutions, the Modernists could bypass the awkward elitism of most of their commissions, presenting them instead as embodying principles for universal application and thereby for progress.

At the same time, Coates worked tirelessly and systematically to bring together what, in 1930, was a rather disparate collection of architects who were progressive to varying degrees, into a tightly knit architectural avant-garde. As its members gradually infiltrated the profession, and other allied institutions, it also won over to the modernist cause the emerging generation of architecture students, who, in turn, would act as an increasingly powerful lobby group for the new architecture. A catalyst for both these processes was the project which, five years after architect and clients first met, became the flats at Lawn Road, Belsize Park, North London.

Lawn Road Flats

The scheme had its origins when, in early 1929, John Craven Pritchard (1899–1992), known as Jack, who ran the Building Uses Department of the plywood manufacturer and importer Venesta Ltd, became aware that a hitherto unknown architect was

opposite: The opening ceremony at the Lawn Road Flats, 9 July 1934. Among those watching Thelma Cazalet, MP for East Islington, are, from second left, Jack and Molly Pritchard and son Jeremy. Wells Coates stands behind Cazalet while the Pritchards' older son, Jonathan, leans over the parapet

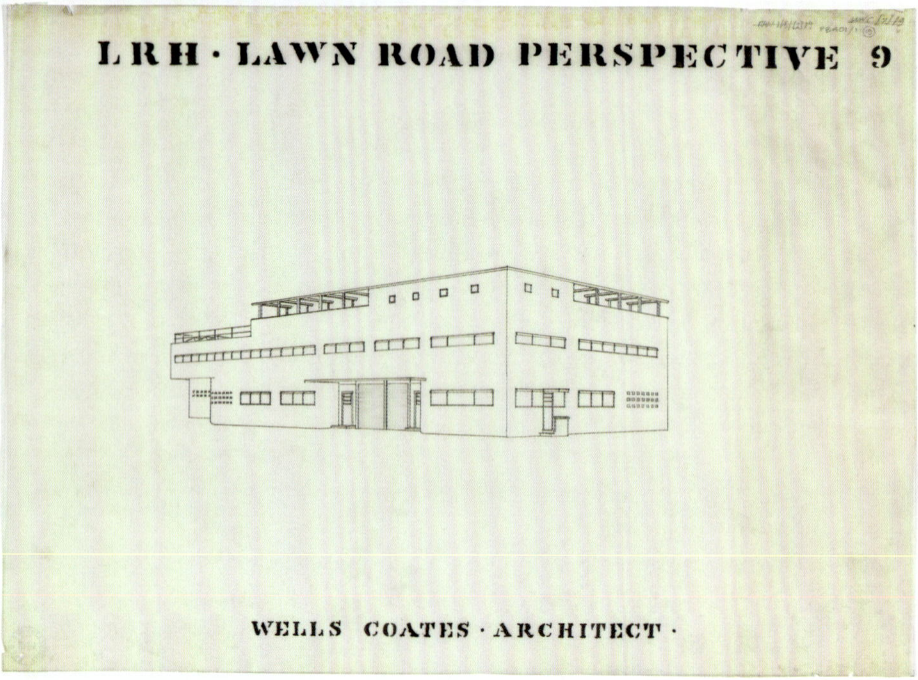

making innovative use of plywood in the interiors of the Crysède chain of shops. A letter was duly dispatched to enquire whether some photographs of this work might be supplied to Venesta for a portfolio the company was assembling to promote the use of its materials to architects. This epistolary encounter brought together two of the most advanced men of the day. Pritchard was a graduate in engineering and economics at Cambridge, and had trained in the techniques of scientific management and market research in his first job at the Michelin Tyre Company in France, before moving, in 1925, to Venesta. In this role he had quickly become aware of the potential for links between designers and manufacturers, and joined the Design and Industries Association (DIA), which had been formed in 1915 to further the contacts between these two constituencies in order to improve the competitiveness and quality of British manufactured goods. By the late 1920s, it had become the main gathering ground for those interested in progressive ideas about design in Britain; Pritchard's membership, and the knowledge it brought him about Modernism both at home and abroad, gave him, he recalled, the 'confidence to experiment with new ideas'.[1]

Initially, Pritchard probably viewed Coates as someone with whom Venesta might collaborate profitably on the lines advocated by the DIA. For Coates, however, his career only just beginning, Pritchard represented more: not just a potential source of publicity

above: **Design for a pair of houses at Lawn Road, *c.* 1930–1**

and, perhaps, work, but, very quickly, a new comrade – a latter-day Borgeaud – with whom he could continue his quest to research and refine his architecture. He later told Pritchard, 'from the moment that I met you I knew instinctively that we were destined to do a job of work in this world, together, someday.'[2]

That 'job' started sooner than he might have anticipated. In the same year, 1929, Jack and his equally progressive wife, Rosemary (1900–85), known as Molly, a doctor turned psychotherapist, had bought a plot of land on Lawn Road, Belsize Park, with the aim of building a house for them and their two young sons. Although they had already commissioned a design from Molly's architect sister and brother-in-law, their growing understanding of modernist principles via the DIA, and their friendship with Coates, led them, by the end the year, to abandon this scheme and commission him to design their home instead.[3] It was during the process of working out precisely the sort of house that they wanted that this small, one-off, project evolved into something much more ambitious.

The reason for this lay in the architect's and clients' approach to the design of the new house, summarised later by Molly as the fateful question: 'How do we want to live, what sort of framework must we build round ourselves to make that living as pleasant as possible?'[4] Thus before any designs were drawn, the three embarked first on several months of discussion about the nature of 'home', studying both British and overseas architecture periodicals, and reading the work of Le Corbusier and Bruno Taut. In April 1930 they visited the Weissenhof Siedlung in Stuttgart, a built catalogue of European modernist approaches to the dwelling. Although Coates went on to produce two sets of designs in this period, the principal outcome of this activity was a growing sense that the kind of work they had seen in continental Europe – which ranged from dwellings for the haute bourgeoisie to homes for the ordinary worker, and incorporated the latest technologies of building and equipment – was simply not possible in Britain. As Pritchard explained, there seemed to be:

> something radically wrong with the organization of building, the main cause being that the architect has been working at pretty exteriors instead of designing according to function on the one hand and according to the material available on the other; while the builder has been so frightened at anything new ... that whenever anything new comes he multiplies the estimate by five and kills the project.[5]

Could their project, then, form the basis of a bigger scheme, one which offered an alternative to the usual methods and outputs of the speculative builder who so dominated the British housing market?

It took the Pritchards and Coates about 18 months from the summer of 1930 to work out fully the form such a scheme might take, but by December 1931, a company, Isokon Ltd, had been formed, with Coates as its Consultant Architect. Isokon (a conflation of Isometric – the engineer's favoured mode of representation – and Unit Construction) would bring the most up-to-date technologies into the

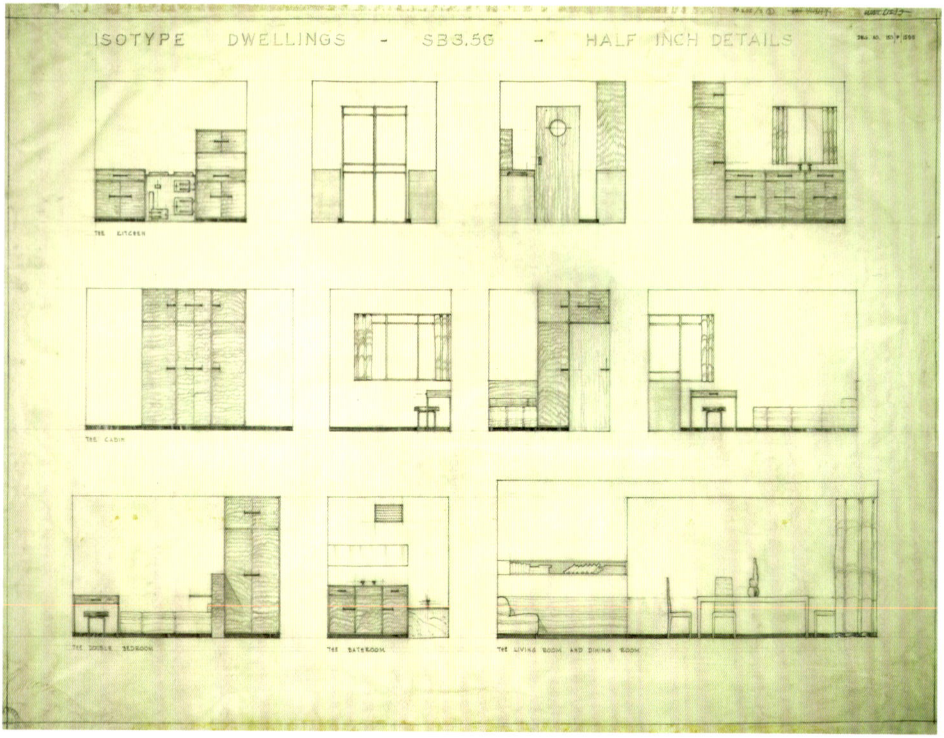

top: Design for Isotype dwelling, *c.* 1932

above: Pencil drawing of built in furniture for the Isotype house, *c.* 1932

speculative building trade in order to show that 'a really scientific house [could] be made' and sold at a low price.[6] Coates's role was to develop the system of 'modern unit construction' which would do this. He therefore developed a series of pre-made component parts that could be combined in various ways to create a series of prefabricated house types, which were to be called 'Isotypes'.[7] Alongside this, a range of standardised furniture for the dwellings would also be developed.

Originally, it was intended that the Pritchards' house would be an Isotype; however, at some point during 1930 or 1931, a new idea emerged from their discussions about the form a modern house might take and, in particular, the location of the site that the Pritchards owned. Given the contemporary concern about the spread of the city into the countryside, Molly asked if it were appropriate to build a house for one family on a central urban site? Would it not be better to build a block of flats, incorporating one for their family.[8] Further discussion ensued, but this proposal was in time agreed and Isokon became a company which, at least in theory, would offer modernist alternatives for all modes of contemporary domestic architecture, whether in the city or the suburb. As things turned out, the suburban model, as discussed below, would take a rather different form from the Isotype, and, renamed Sunspan, be produced by another company. Isokon would survive the decade as a furniture manufacturer but its sole building project would be the flat prototype, which, named the Lawn Road Flats, opened in June 1934.[9]

The form of this prototype was influenced by a number of factors. Given that the intention was to provide a viable alternative to the speculative market, one proviso was that the new block should be distinctly different, and better, than the emerging type of urban flat, which offered serviced accommodation invariably within a Neo-Georgian exterior. Hence, the Pritchards looked to Coates to produce an equivalent block which contained a number of service flats, each with large living room, kitchenette, bathroom or bath–dressing room, facilities for a bed space, dressing space and dining space, but which did so cheaply and which in turn produced a standardised unit or units that could be repeated easily.[10] They also defined their target market as a type of person still somewhat overlooked by the speculator: the modern professional, male or female (the latter consideration, another marker of the project's progressive nature), who more usually had to settle for 'rooms' in a converted house, without a private bathroom or cooking facilities but invariably with a fearsome landlady. By April 1933, a budget of approximately £13,500 had been agreed and 29 flats plus staff accommodation and penthouse for the couple and their children specified. The contract price was later pared down to £12,500, while the project eventually cost £14,850.

To the realisation of this basic set of parameters, Coates brought two main themes. First, in keeping with the principle that these should be definitively modern flats, there was his particular conception of the inhabitant of each dwelling unit as a figure very similar to himself and his Fitzrovian friends. This was a modern 'type' created by the modern age. He wrote:

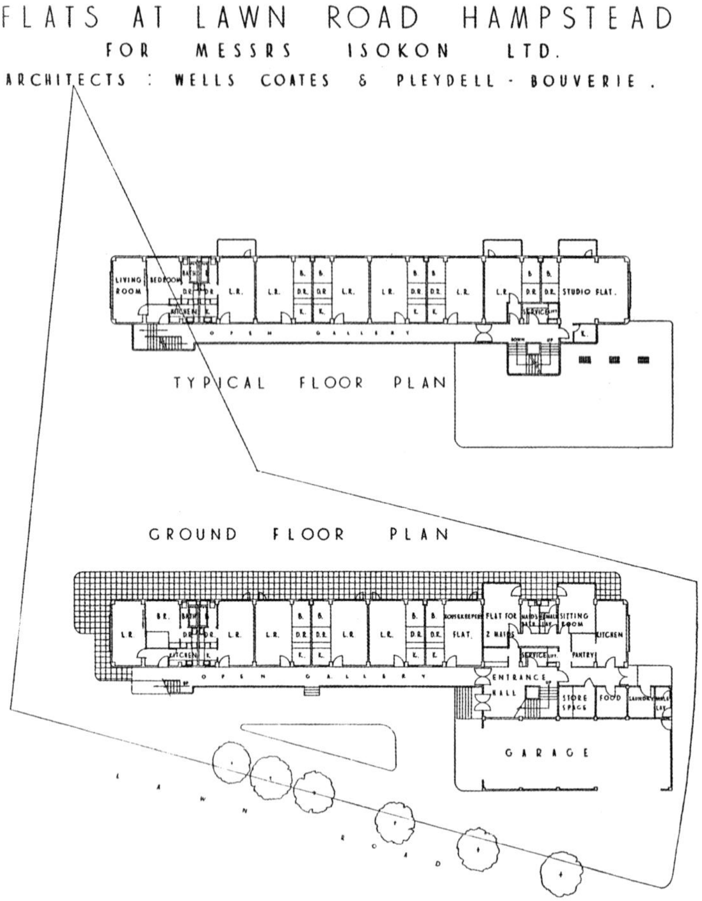

Our society is above all determined to be free. The love of travel and change, the mobility of the worker himself, grows with every opportunity to indulge it. The 'home' is no longer a permanent place from one generation to another ... we move away from the old home and family; we get rid of our belongings and make for a new exciting freedom. A new freedom which demands a greater comfort and a more perfect order and repose, also a new type of intricacy in the equipment of the dwelling-scene.[11]

Second, from his reading of Keyserling came the idea that 'a room exists for the man, and not vice versa, that he, and not the curtain or the picture is to be given the

top: **Plans of Lawn Road Flats, indicating site boundary**

best possible setting.'[12] Thus Coates conceived of the block, in Molly's words, as a series of frameworks, comprising the plan, the equipment and the servicing of the flats as a whole, which connected to each resident and thereby enabled them to live freely and well. At the same time, he produced a rigorously standardised design of three type plans – for a single-room 'minimum' flat, a double flat and a studio flat – the whole to be built from monolithic reinforced concrete in order for it to be as cheap, and replicable, as possible.

As built, the block comprised four, gallery-accessed storeys. Each contained a larger 'double' flat at the south end and, from first- to third-floor level, five standard minimum flats plus a double-size studio flat entered next to the stairs and lift. The Pritchards' apartment topped the block and comprised a main flat with smaller annex for their

above left: **Interior of the Dorland Hall Minimum Flat, showing built-in fitment and bed**

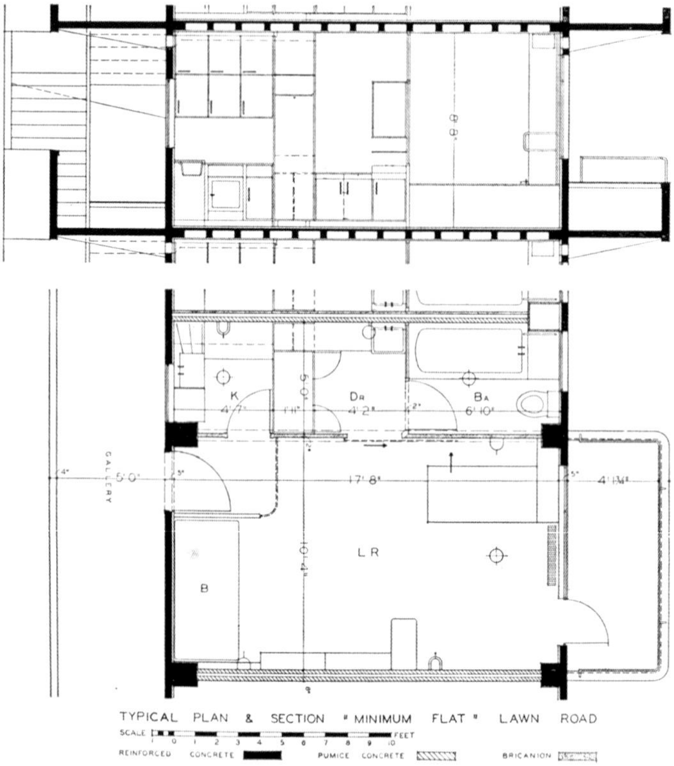

top: Section and plan of the Minimum Flat at Lawn Road Flats

above: View of interior of Minimum Flat. This is the prototype exhibited at Dorland Hall, 1933

boys. At ground-floor level were placed three staff flats with kitchen and laundry to serve the residents, space which was later converted into the Isobar, a social club, designed by F. R. S. Yorke and Marcel Breuer (who lived at Lawn Road when he came to England from Nazi Germany). The Pritchards' choice of architect for this latter commission reflected, as will become apparent, the deterioration in relationships between them and Coates once the flats were completed in 1934.

Coates derived the formal appearance of the block from its structure. This had been determined by the fact that two railway tunnels ran directly underneath each end of the site, requiring him to use a system of construction that could cantilever the extremities of the building over the tunnels. This provided him with his design motif, in the dramatically projecting access balconies to each gallery. It would become a favourite device, writ large at Embassy Court, and echoed, in miniature,

above: **View of Lawn Road flats after restoration completed in 2004. The dramatic lighting of the balconies follows the original style**

in the external staircases at Shipwrights and The Homewood. A second influence was his choice of monolithic reinforced concrete (its render tinted a light pink) for the structure. This was a construction system of far greater complexity than the more standard frame-and-infill technique used by many of his contemporaries. Whereas that system was almost invariably expressed in a rectilinear form, with its component parts clearly articulated, the monolithic system, which formed frame and wall together, encouraged the conceptualisation and formation of the building as a seamless, sculptural whole.

Within the block the 'minimum' was the dominant flat type. In this, the real advantages of the Isokon prototype became evident, as Coates solved brilliantly, and with real insight, the problem of how to design a small space in which to live well (the main living area is 5.4 m x 3.15 m [18 x 10 feet], the whole 5.4 m x 4.67 m [18 x 15 feet]). A starting point for this process was the fact that the floor-to-ceiling heights of the interiors were taller than usual for the period. This allowed a greater 'throw' to the window in a room which was single-aspect, as well as an enhanced sense of headroom. Within that shell, every square inch of space was accounted for and put to use. Built-in furniture demarcated the living and sleeping areas of the main room, sliding doors separated the 'service' strip of rooms in the flat, and its tiny kitchen (1.4 m x 1.52 m [4½ x 5 feet]) was planned around the arm-reach of its user. A significant example of Coates's ability to design space may be seen in the incorporation of the dressing room into the plan. At first glance this might be considered to be unnecessary, yet without it the actualities of daily living would be the more difficult: the act of dressing is out of place in a living room, and uncomfortable in a bathroom. Here, then, was space as equipment, facilitating and ritualising the transition from being at home to venturing into the world at large.[13] Such facilities also distinguished the flats at Lawn Road from mere bedsits, further enhancing their appeal to the professionals at whom the block was aimed: as Jack later recalled, 'Without such facilities it would be like a bed-sitter with nowhere to keep clothing. The bed would also act as a couch.'[14]

The idea of the block as a supporting framework did not just reside in the planning of each flat but also in its servicing. Depending on the rent paid – between £96 and £170 per annum – tenants were entitled to services which ranged from daily bed-making and cleaning to the provision of meals. The integral nature of these services further explains the small size of the flats: the tiny kitchens were not intended to be used for the production of elaborate dinner parties or, indeed, evening meals. This was the function of the kitchen on the ground floor, from which food could be ordered by a quick telephone call; such provision mattered at a time when it was unusual for middle-class professionals, especially men, to have any cooking skills.[15] More generally, Coates and the Pritchards were working from the funda-

previous pages: **The Pritchards' living room in their penthouse flat, from *Decorative Art, the Studio Year Book*, 1936**

mental premise that for the modern man or woman home was only a backdrop to a life lived largely in the public realm.

It is worth remembering that Coates was working on 1KPG at the same time that he began the design of Lawn Road, and it is evident how many of the devices used in that elite interior were transposed to a block intended for a relatively more ordinary set of clients. The built-in wall fitment echoed that in the living room of the Kensington mansion, and included both an electric fire and combined wireless and cocktail cabinet, and Coates again used sliding rather than hinged doors to separate interior spaces. Each flat enjoyed a similar level of technological specification, with ample provision of lighting and a kitchen which included an electric refrigerator, while the service lift that delivered meals from the ground-floor kitchen to a hatch on each floor was a democratised form of the dumb waiter that emerged into the Kensington dining room from the kitchen below.

Molly Pritchard would pick up on this idea of disseminating the benefits of progress in her speech on the opening day of the flats, declaring, 'the intention of ISOKON [*sic*] is to provide ... "good living" for as many people as possible. If this block is a success and we make money on it, we shall use that money for building another block and so on. In fact we hope to be able to have a chain of this kind of flats over the country.'[16] While this proved to be optimistic, the fact that the block represented something significant and imitable is apparent in the response of the journalist, and later Director of the Festival of Britain, Gerald Barry, who observed, 'the experiment is the signpost to a new order – it represents in concrete and steel the new attitude towards this business of living which is beginning to emerge from our present-day chaos.'[17]

Even before the block had been completed, care had been taken to promote the design. In May 1933, Coates took part in a BBC wireless discussion, later published in the *Listener*, entitled 'Modern Dwellings for Modern Needs', in which he expounded many of the ideas explored at Lawn Road.[18] The following month, a full-scale mock-up of the minimum flat was displayed at the Exhibition of British Industrial Art in the Home, held at Dorland Hall in Regent Street, London. Widely reported and praised, the exhibit not only attracted sufficient down payments to allow the scheme to be finalised, but, it also seems likely, drew other speculators' attention to Lawn Road as a prototype. Away from the specifics of the brief, it was an exercise in the development of different levels of accommodation within one overall scheme, with attendant detail paid to their integration into a system of extensive servicing. It was Coates's ability to juggle these demands which, perhaps, encouraged a firm of developers, Maddox Properties Ltd, to approach him to work with them on a scheme – Embassy Court – planned for the seafront at Brighton. It would seem that they were dissatisfied with initial plans that they had had drawn up by the firm of Bertram Carter and Sloot, and which had been published in 1933.[19]

Embassy Court

A much bigger project than Lawn Road, the site was on the main promenade, King's Road, on the boundary between boisterous, populist Brighton and the separate, and much quieter and more genteel, municipality of Hove. The plot abutted Amon Wild's Brunswick Terrace, and had been occupied by a Regency town house which had been demolished some years previously. Following a deal with the local authority, which wanted to widen and tidy up the road junction around the site, Maddox was able to proceed with plans for what it described as a 'mansion' block,[20] 11 storeys high, aimed at the 'professional and business classes'.[21]

The commission offered Coates the opportunity to continue and develop his quest to resolve the problem of the appropriate setting for the 'theatre' of modern life, and the block should be understood as a series of permutations on themes first worked out at Lawn Road, albeit with a more complex programme and a less parsimonious budget. So whereas the Pritchards had required three plan types, Coates produced seven for Maddox. These ranged from one-bed (with or without dressing-room recess), reception room, kitchen and bathroom, to three beds, two reception rooms, two bathrooms and a kitchen. The apartments were arranged in combination on each floor to enable a variety of rents to be charged (from £120 to £500 per annum, not including service costs) in order to attract the widest possible range of wealthy residents to this premium seafront block.

above: **Period postcard view of Embassy Court in its Regency setting**

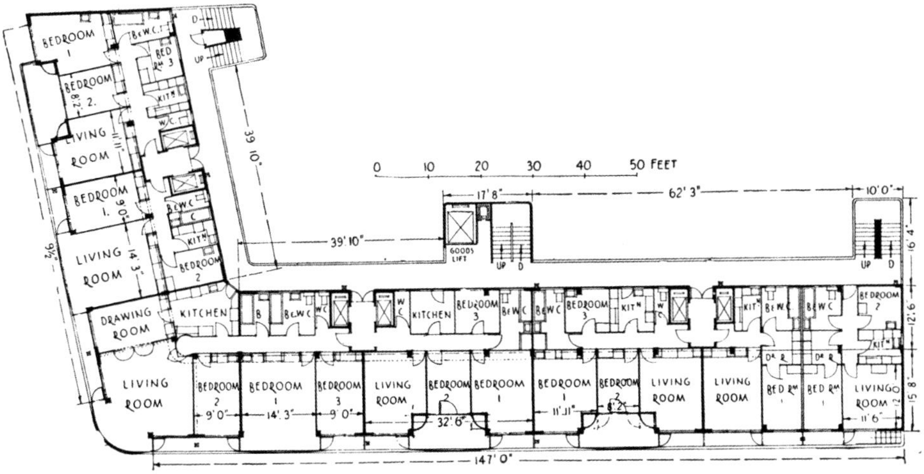

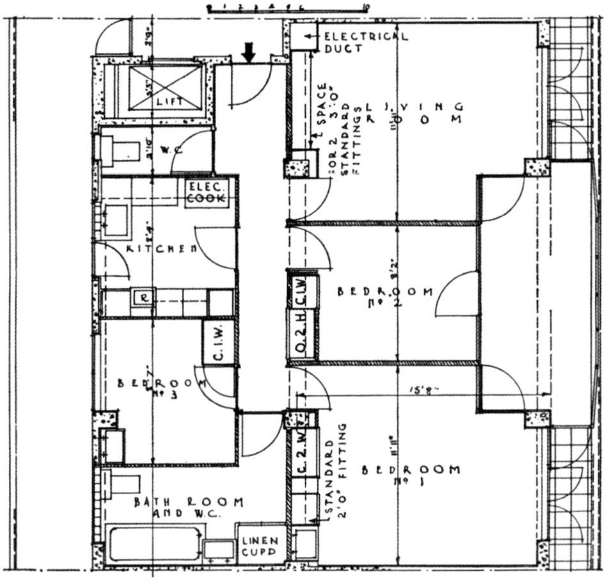

top: **Plan of a typical floor of Embassy Court**
above: **Plan of a typical flat at Embassy Court**

TAXIS ONLY

top: The main entrance of Embassy Court
above: The photo-mural designed by Edward McKnight Kauffer for the foyer of Embassy Court
previous pages: Embassy Court, after restoration in 2006

Regardless of the number of the rooms, Coates adopted a standard format for each flat type, the chief determinant of which was a distinction between what the architect Louis Kahn later termed 'served and servant spaces' (a separation made on a smaller scale at Lawn Road). At Embassy Court, the main residents' spaces of living and bedrooms were arranged in sequence to face front (south, or south-east), with a set-back, enclosed, sunroom accessible from all the rooms, glazed with 'Vita sun glass' that did not block out any of the ultraviolet rays then believed to be health-giving and harmless: the first use of the material in this context, so the sales brochure proclaimed. A narrow enclosed balcony either side of the sunroom completed this suite of spaces. As at Lawn Road, a set of specially designed furniture, built-in and freestanding, was available for purchase. To underline the separation of the primary rooms from the 'back of house', Coates used a spine corridor, opening directly from the front door. The resulting strip comprised the one or more bathrooms and WCs and the kitchen, for which Coates designed the most astonishing, and surely largely unreachable, fitted unit.

Residents reached their flats having entered the block through its splendid chrome entrance doors, and moved into the plush communal foyer and thence to the lifts. The foyer contained a porter's desk, as well as tables and chairs, all to Coates's design, and also featured a photo-mural, which depicted Brightonian and maritime themes, designed by Edward McKnight Kauffer, his collaborator at Cresta. The 'structural' quality of this apparent form of decoration should be noted. It was produced by a new technique, patented by Eugene Mollo, through which a design was projected onto a surface coated with photosensitive paint. On drying, the image thus formed an integral part of the wall: a structural seamlessness akin to that of the monolithic method of

above: **The living room of the Embassy Court show flat**

construction used for the block as a whole. A similar integration may be found in the block's heating system. This was provided by an innovative system of storage panels, the coils for which were embedded into the concrete structure as it went up. Although it probably only saved a few centimetres in terms of the space otherwise occupied by a radiator, and space was not at such a premium as at Lawn Road (here, the largest living rooms were 4.5 m x 5.7 m [15 x 18½ feet]), the effortlessness of the heating added to the overall sense of luxury befitting a mansion block.

Again, each flat was conceived of as 'wired into' the block as a whole, both spatially and through the provision of a network of services. While residents came and went through the front doors of both block and flat, their staff (whether their own or those available for daily hire from the in-house service) used an entirely separate circulation system which was reached from the kitchen door of each flat. This took the servant onto the rear access balconies which ran across the rear elevation and then down (or up) to the ground-floor kitchen or basement garages, or to their accommodation (basement for chauffeurs, roof level for the maids). A maid service was available on an hourly paid basis, providing, the developers claimed, the facilities of a service flat without the permanent charges, and it was also possible to have meals prepared and sent upstairs (many of the kitchens being, therefore, commensurately small).

The structure which enclosed and supported this network of served and servant spaces was, like Lawn Road, a cantilevered monolithic reinforced-concrete frame (this time with a cream-tint render, which contained chips of marble or mica and which

above: **The sun room**

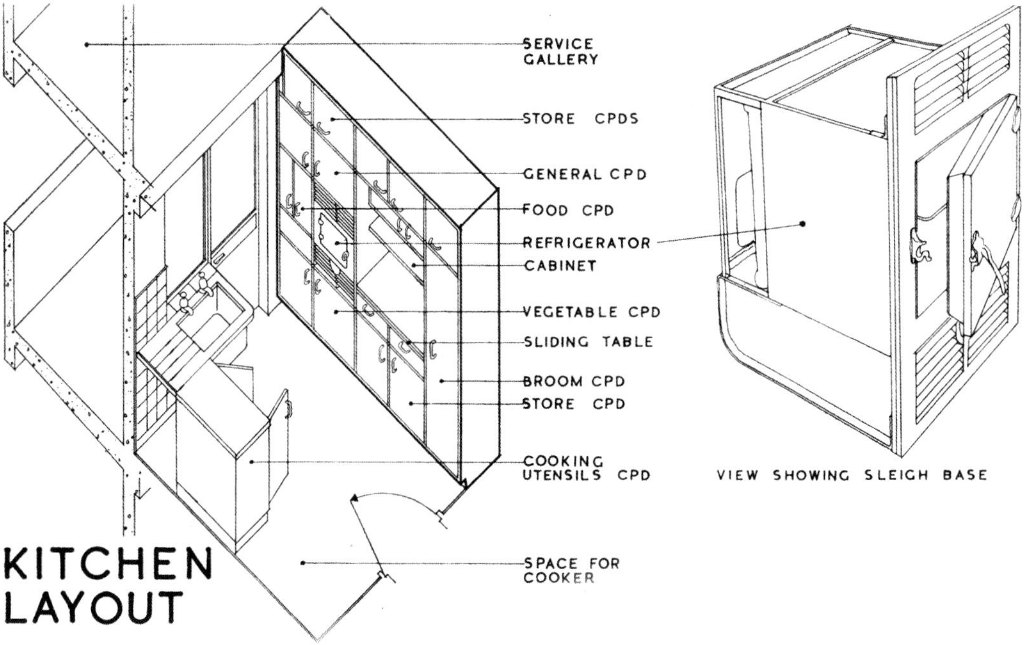

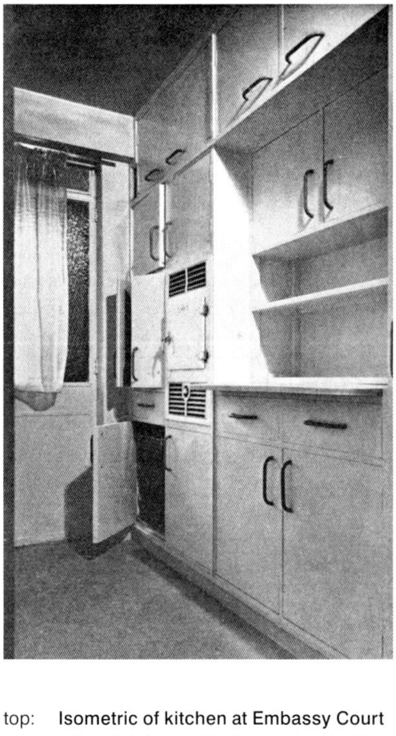

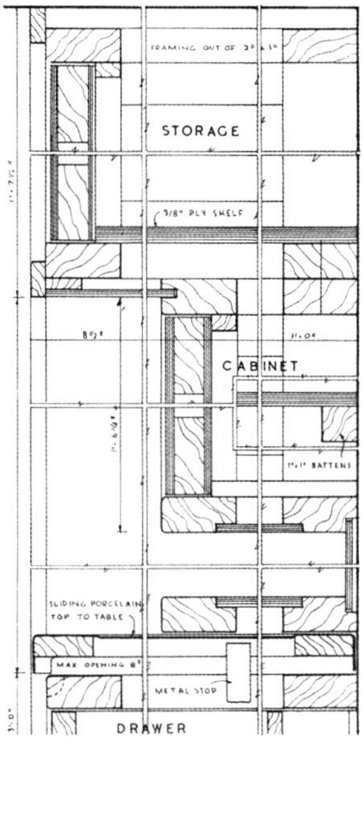

top: **Isometric of kitchen at Embassy Court**

above left: **Kitchen at Embassy Court; right: section of cupboard**

would therefore have glistened slightly in the sun). The three lift shafts and three staircase towers provided added bracing to the frame. The voluptuous balconies which had formed the design motif at Lawn Road were, at Embassy Court, migrated to the rear for programmatic reasons, thus creating surely one of the best backs of a building in architectural history. For the main elevations, the horizontal theme was retained, but here the cantilevers were contained within the flush wall surface which enclosed the strip windows of the sun rooms.

Both Lawn Road and Embassy Court were reported in all the main architectural periodicals, not just the resolutely pro-modernist *Architects' Journal* and *Architectural Review* but also the more eclectically minded *Building* and *Architect and Building News*. For C. H. Reilly, one of the leading critics and architects of the day, the block was among the best of the year's buildings. He described it as a 'tall graceful building with its long clean lines, vertical as well as horizontal, its fragile-looking romantic staircases with landing above landing cantilevered out against the sky, and night and day thrilling one to the marrow', concluding that 'Everyone should see it'. Significantly, Reilly linked the effectiveness of the design to Coates's engineering background, noting, 'If this is the result of a mathematical training and a Ph.D ... the architectural courses in our schools must be altered at once.'[22]

The two schemes also captured a more popular audience. Coates's press-cuttings book has clippings from the *Yorkshire Post* to the *Spectator* for Lawn Road, while Embassy Court inspired a vision of the future for Sir Herbert Carden, the Brighton Alderman. Addressing a town meeting in February 1935, just as the block was going up, he spoke of his dream to tear down the whole of the rest of King's Road 'from one end to the other ... replacing it with similar buildings to the flats of Embassy Court'.[23]

Well-received Lawn Road and Embassy Court may have been, but for the always restless and inventive Coates, they were but stages in the development of the definitive form of modern dwelling; a desire to research an optimum solution to the need for decent housing for all which also reflected his formation of the MARS Group (see below) and its concern to resolve contemporary architectural problems. Each scheme had also, in varying ways, been the victims of compromise which meant the resulting buildings were not quite the efficient machines that Coates had in mind. At Lawn Road, for example, the Pritchards' inexperience, and their tight budget, caused skimping on the finishing of the building; decisions whose legacy was an endless saga of leaky roofs and condensation problems. At Embassy Court, the developer's decision to include the unique feature of the sunroom meant that the balconies were too narrow to hold a chair because no more space could be taken from the main suite of rooms. The challenge for the architect remained therefore, as Coates explained in an article written for the *Architectural Review* in August 1937, to produce a design model which allowed the developers their profit but which did so in a way that produced satisfactory domestic spaces that were also complete works of architecture.[24]

opposite: **Rear staircase and access galleries at Embassy Court**

The article continued with Coates's first ideas on how to move on from the developer's model. Likely influenced, at least conceptually, by Moise Ginzburg's and Ignatii Milinis's Narkomfin apartment block in Moscow (1929-30), a scheme of duplex flats, accessed from an internal 'street', instead of the standard programme of apartments all on one floor, he proposed a basic system of a '3-2' unit in which three floors on one side of a block of flats were equal to two floors on the other, so that two flats interlocked in the height of three floors. At the middle level would be placed one or two 'corridors': one open gallery for service and access to the escape stairs, the other an internal corridor (a permutation of the Embassy Court theme of the separation of the space occupied by those who served and were served). From the corridor one would either go up half a storey to the flat at the upper level, or down a full storey to that at the lower. This basic arrangement had the advantage for the developer of reducing circulation space and limiting the number of lift stops (with lifts stopping at alternate floors only), thereby lowering costs and increasing the space available for flats. But Coates also provided a further innovation, proposing that within this system it would also be possible for the basic 3-2 unit to be expanded by borrowing space from units to the side. Claiming that it was possible for 'as many as forty variations, forty different arrangements of rooms' to be produced, although his exposition for this was rather unclear, in theory it meant that

top: John Piper, preparatory sketch for the 'Regency-Victorian-Modern' print for the 1939 book, *Brighton Aquatints,* showing Embassy Court in context. Piper gave the drawing to Coates as a gift

the developer essentially had a kit of parts. Thus, as he wrote, 'the tenant who asks what type of flats you have is answered: "what type do you want?"'

If the intricacies of the design satisfied Coates's engineering instincts, the technique of planning-in-section also created a more ceremonial aspect to the modern interior. Invoking the Great Halls of the pre-Renaissance house, with all their connotations of

top: **Perspective of unrealised scheme for flats, Ivor Court, Bristol, 1937 with interiors showing the 3-2 system**

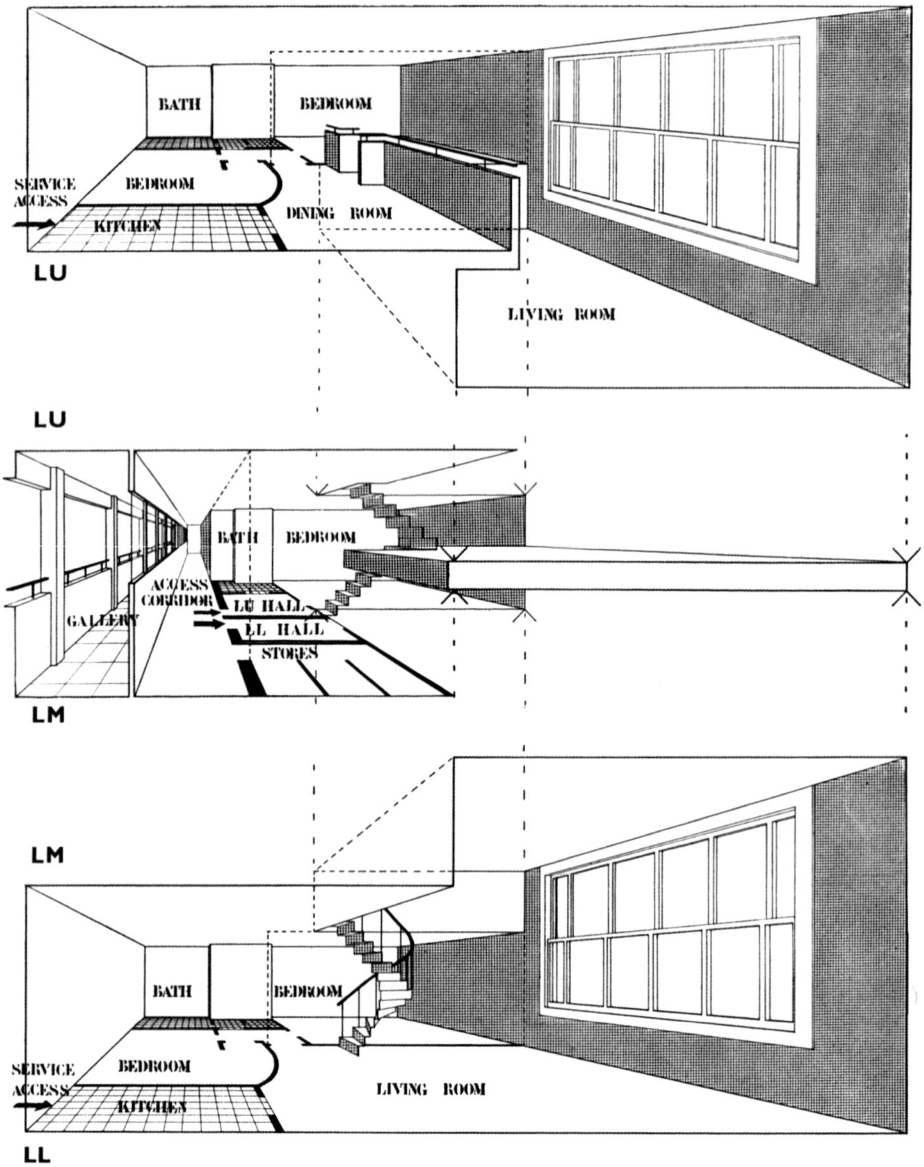

communal gathering and entertainment, Coates made the focus of each unit a generously dimensioned double-height living area, in the mezzanine of which was sited the dining area.[25] This rhetorical use of space was something Coates had struggled to achieve in the plans at Lawn Road and Embassy Court, perhaps relying on the fact

above: **The 3-2 planning system as executed at 10 Palace Gate**

that their occupants were more likely to be out on the town than spending evenings at home. The 3-2 unit, by contrast, influenced in part by his growing experience of designing complete houses (Shipwrights was being planned at this time) was arguably more of an attempt to translate the experience of the house into a vertically stacked, central urban context. Coates would later explain to student interior designers what he was striving to achieve in this expanded use of space:

> You must remember that as interior designers you have to plan for use, first, but you also plan for delight. Dimensions here are perhaps fourth dimensions, at any rate the problem is not merely three-dimensional. And you will find what colour, texture, the type of lighting, whether artificial or natural; the selection of your materials and the way you organise them, you will find what all these will do to dimensions.[26]

The article was illustrated with drawings of a proposed scheme at Bristol incorporating the 3-2 apartments, which was never realised (but which, perhaps, had been a further motivation to work through new ideas about the optimum form of urban dwelling). The work was not wasted, however, for, some time in early 1937, a chance meeting at a cocktail party with a young property developer, Randal Bell, provided him with the opportunity to realise the concept on a grand scale. A week after this encounter, Bell visited Coates at Yeoman's Row (the interior of which was, of course, a live prototype of the individual apartments) and listened as the architect described the 3-2 section and a new site he had identified, at Palace Gate (close by Hyde Park) on which to build. Much to Coates's surprise – Bell recalled he thought he would fall off his chair – the developer agreed to build and within six weeks ground was being broken on the site.[27] 10 Palace Gate would be completed in early 1939.

10 Palace Gate

Bell was the ideal client for Coates, able to put the reins on when necessary but also enlightened enough to allow his architect to create architecture rather than a piece of space designed for profit. Thus he vetoed Coates's preferred building skin of concrete on grounds of crazing and maintenance costs; a decision which led Coates to develop instead a system of artificial stone cladding which did not require scaffolding and resulted in an exterior more suited to a location in close proximity to Hyde Park.

Like Embassy Court, 10 Palace Gate was a luxury block, though not serviced to the same extent as the Brighton scheme, and the flats were sufficiently large to accommodate live-in staff. It comprises two blocks. The western entrance block was planned conventionally, with single level flats on each floor (at rents of £175 a year). It interconnected via the stair/lift tower to the rear block which contains three sets of 3-2 units (containing two, three and four bedrooms, their rents ranging from £310 to £425 annually) topped by a penthouse and extensive roof terrace. In keeping with the principles outlined in his article of 1937, the flats were entered from an internal corridor or service gallery, which were sited at alternate levels, from ground floor up, across the

six storeys of the blocks. The flat interiors were furnished with Coates's usual carefully choreographed set of built-in furniture and fittings.

As well as creating interiors of satisfying proportions, the 3-2 arrangement created exteriors of great formal quality. The interplay of the void of the service galleries against the 3-section screen walls on the front elevation, and the tapering of the columns towards the top of the block, signal the building's structure while the extension of the roof line of the penthouse to form the roof pergola achieves a satisfying junction as the building meets the sky. The rear elevation, with the windows of the living spaces fully articulated, again offers a clear statement of the interior organisation. If there is a touch of homage to Le Corbusier's Pavillon Suisse, Paris (1930–31) in the stone-faced facades and the concavity of the entrance block, the scheme as whole, especially viewed alongside Shipwrights and the Homewood, nevertheless represents the ongoing evolution of Coates's architectural language, an important reminder that for him Modernism could never be a style, but was always a response to a specific set of circumstances and programmatic demands. No wonder that a critic noted, 'Palace Gate now shelters an architectural work of contemporary significance'.[28]

above: The concave entrance block contains single-height flats and the main lift and stairs. The flanking wings show service access galleries at every third level, with service stairs at the ends
opposite: The east-facing façade shows the large windows of the double-height rooms with the smaller bedroom windows to the sides.

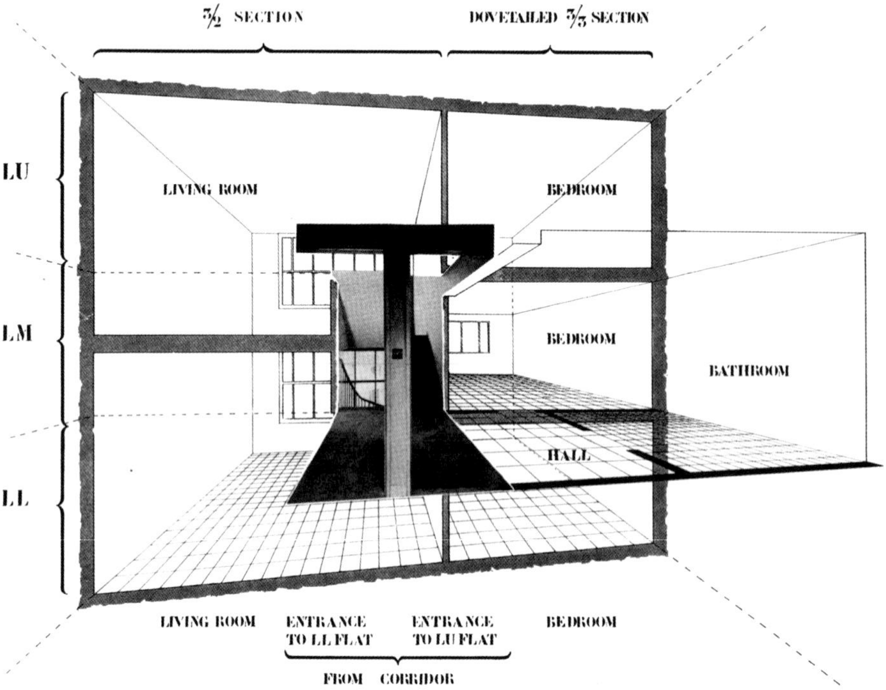

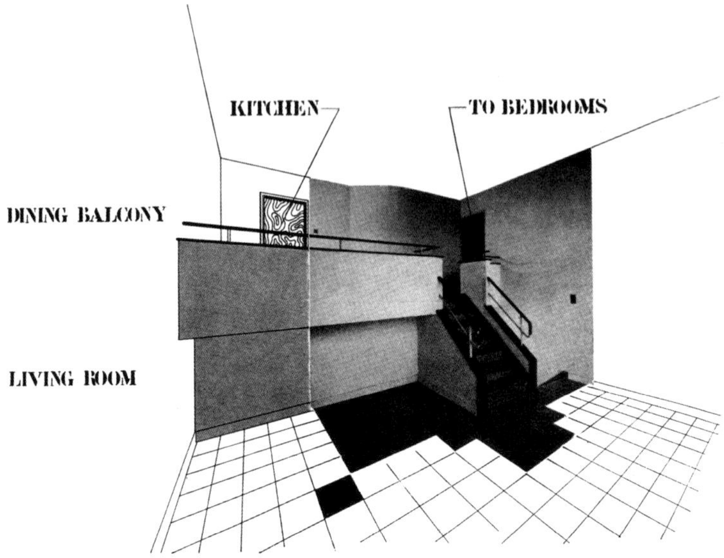

above: **Explanatory photomontages of the 3-2 system as used at 10 Palace Gate**

The 'Isotype House' and 'Sunspan'

If the Brighton, Belsize Park and Palace Gate schemes brought Coates's Modernism to a wider, but by no means mass, market, another offspring of the Isokon project promised more. At the same time as Coates and his office were working on these projects, he had also found the time to develop and realise the Isotype house idea. This, however, was not achieved with the Pritchards but with a speculative builder, E. & L. Berg Ltd. Coates's motivations for working with someone else can only be imagined, but they do reveal a ruthless streak to his nature, when the chance to get something done outweighed the proprieties of friendship and conscience. Certainly, relationships with the Pritchards had grown increasingly strained as the Lawn Road project reached fruition. Their focus on flats alone may also have frustrated Coates, because his zeal for the modernist cause provided him with the boundless energy to pursue every possible opening for its promulgation that came his way. Thus, when Berg offered the opportunity to put a version of the Isotype suburban house into production – presumably to cash in on the fashion for 'Modernistic' houses then emerging – he grabbed it.

A little to his credit, Coates was not crass enough to simply replicate the Isotype format. So while the principle of a set of designs for component parts remained, these were to be made up into a range of more compact house types, from what was described, rather anachronistically, as a cottage, to a large five-bedroomed house.[29] These were to be constructed from Lewis dovetail steel sheeting, a frame-and-panel system which comprised 50 mm (two inch) pipe columns sandwiched between a double membrane of steel. This was then rendered externally with cement, internally with plaster, and had a tarmacadam flat roof. Their defining feature, and hence the catchy name 'Sunspan', derived from the fact that the house was oriented so that each corner was at a compass point, resulting in a main living space with windows on both south-

above: **Sketch of imagined interior of the 10 Palace Gate penthouse, by Gordon Cullen**

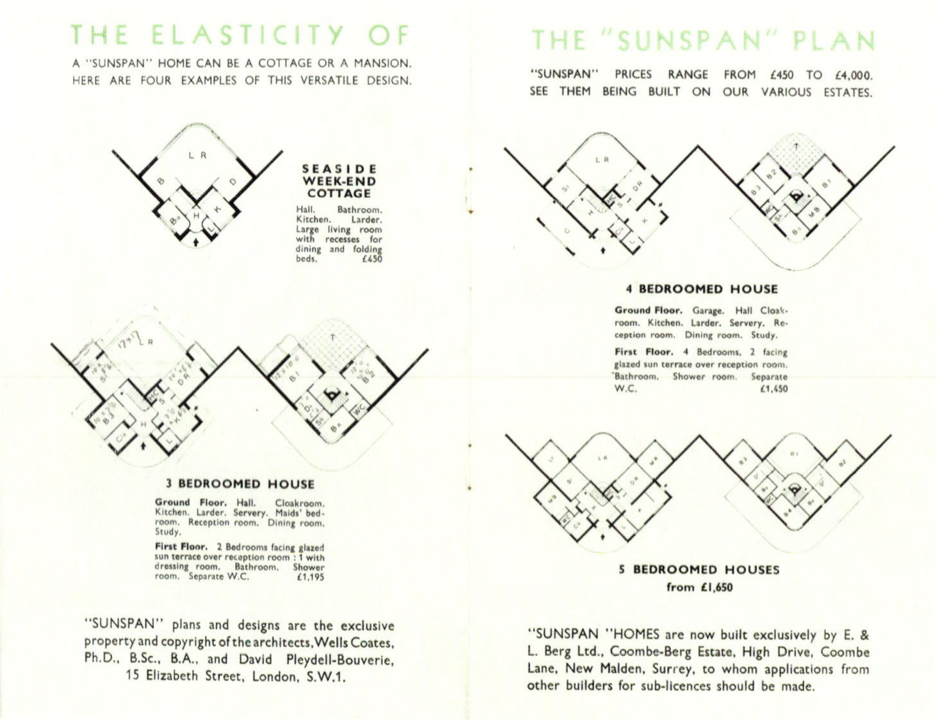

east and south-west elevations, ensuring direct sunlight into this room at all times of the day.

A prototype Sunspan house (three bedrooms plus one for the maid) costing £1,495 made its debut at the 1934 *Daily Mail* Ideal Home Exhibition as part of that year's 'Village of Tomorrow'. This, so the catalogue declared, featured 'designs for better living', from builders like Wates and Laings as well as Berg, all of them flat-roofed, white rendered and with large expanses of windows. The Sunspan house stood out from the rest owing to its curvilinear form, and its construction. Perhaps because of this, Berg was anxious to stress that its 'advanced design' did not preclude it from being 'home-like in spirit'. It likewise linked its 'ordered scientific plan' to values an Ideal Home visitor would have found familiar: 'the central idea that home is the place of untrammelled comfort, perpetual ease, increasing delight'.[30]

Such hyperbole might be expected from the promoters of both exhibition and house, but it was paralleled in the *Architects' Journal* declaration of the Sunspan concept as 'perhaps the first serious English contribution to domestic planning since that famous discovery of the "free, open planning" of the English country house took the Continent by storm at the beginning of the century', concluding with a flourish: 'as such it may well prove to be epoch-making'.[31] The magazine based this assessment on the fact that

above: **Sunspan type plans from sales brochure, 1934**

above: The Sunspan house at the *Daily Mail* Ideal Home Exhibition, 1934
top: Master Bedroom of the Sunspan house at the *Daily Mail* Ideal Home Exhibition

the house was a type-plan, which could be scaled up or down according to demand, and because it was the only house in the Village that had been designed, furnished and equipped throughout to an architect's plan.

AN IMPRESSION FROM THE AIR OF "SUNSPAN" HOMES NOW BEING BUILT ON THE
WENTWORTH ESTATE, DITTON HILL, SURBITON, SURREY, BY E. & L. BERG, LTD.
We invite you to visit this estate. Not only to see these different houses, but to enjoy the prospect of a new kind of estate planning. For the "SUNSPAN" PLAN enables an estate to be laid out so that each house is islanded in its own secluded plot.

It is hard to take this view seriously. Flexible the house type may have been, and thanks to the sliding doors between the main ground floor rooms it was possible to open the interior into one large space, but Coates allowed the idea that the house should be open to the sun throughout the day to dominate the design at the expense of rationality. In what was intended to be a mass-produced house, it seems unlikely that a nation still wedded to the idea of the 'front' room would want such an undefined ground-floor area. Coates also sidestepped the matter of how to buy furniture in the High Street for a house with curved walls. Although he did design a range of furniture for the house, this was manufactured by Gordon Russell, not a mass-market supplier by any means.

A client less interested in sensationalism might have stayed their architect's hand, and Sunspan might be best understood as a 'loss-leader' for Berg's range of more conventional houses. Its commitment to the specifics of the design in the wake of the exhibition suggests this. Although an estate of houses at Thames Ditton in Surrey was commissioned, only three of these were built and of the other dozen or so versions that were constructed, only one, a bungalow near Welwyn Garden City, was built from the material originally proposed; the rest were brick, rendered in plaster. Nearly all have been substantially altered.[32]

above: **Plan for an estate of Sunspan houses at Thames Ditton, Surrey, 1934, with houses arranged to prevent overshadowing**

Furniture and Product Design

Coates's relationship with the mass market was not always so negative. A clear sign of the innovative nature of his work was the fact that, as noted in his design for the Crysède store, he could not buy furniture and equipment 'off the peg', instead having to design and detail it himself. While this may sometimes have proved an onerous task, it did lead him to develop a significant career as a furniture and product designer, as designs for specific commissions were patented and, in collaboration with a number of progressive manufacturers, put into batch, if not mass, production. An early example of this process was the D-handle, made from bent steel coated with coloured resin, which was first used at Crysède and then taken up by Taylor Pearse and Company and marketed under the Tayloroid brand. Available in a range of sizes and colours (from black and ivory to terracotta and blue), they became ubiquitous in the interwar modern interior. Likewise, the dining room chairs and the armchair used at 1KPG were quickly replicated, but were aimed at a relatively high-end market through showrooms like that of the interior designer Duncan Miller.

Many of Coates's collaborators were new companies who were the first in the market to use materials and technologies which were either recently invented or now able to be mass-produced. Importantly, they also recognised the benefits of working with designers. This was a sign of the growing influence of the DIA. It marked the true beginning of a consensus in industry, and some parts of government, that design must become an integral part of the manufacturing process if Britain were to regain its position in the world market. Thus during the 1930s, Coates worked extensively with companies like Hilmor Ltd and PEL (Practical Equipment Ltd), which produced much of the furniture for Embassy Court, both of which were leading manufacturers of tubular-steel furniture, a technology which had only come to Britain at the end of the 1920s. He also designed for P. E. Gane Ltd and, of course, Isokon.

above: **Sunspan Bungalow at Mardley Hill, near Welwyn Garden City, 1935**

Such consultancy work helped to reinforce Coates's persona of the architect as expert form giver, and it was exemplified in his most famous collaboration, that with Ekco (E. K. Cole Ltd). Set up in 1926, Ekco not only produced the archetypal piece of modern communications technology – the wireless – but had, since 1930, done so using one of the newest of materials: Bakelite. The decision to use this form of plastic had been taken, so the company's Chief Engineer, John Wyborn, explained, because mass-produced wooden cabinets were prone to warping and it was hard to produce them cheaply to the uniform dimensions the market required.[33] Bakelite, being a material moulded into shape by heat, was inherently uniform and quintessentially a material for mass-production. And although initial costs were high in equipping a factory and having moulds made, labour costs were cheap because no skilled work was involved in the manufacturing process. Nevertheless, the decision to use Bakelite was something of a gamble at a time when most wirelesses were made from wood, and Ekco needed to make sure its investment paid off. Thus when its first plastic set failed to reach sales target, and it was discovered that this was principally because of a lack of 'sales appeal in the Bakelite cabinet', Wyborn had to think again.

The problem was that Bakelite as a material lacked what he called the 'interest' inherent in the grain of a wood; as such, a plastic case that merely reproduced a wooden cabinet design would be inherently inferior. Yet, Bakelite had the advantage that, because it was mouldable, it could take forms that wood could not. Wyborn concluded, 'It is by its superior "form", therefore, that the plastic cabinet must make up for its lack of interest as a material.' And from this realisation came another. The in-house engineering office was not capable of designing such forms, as the poor sales of the first plastic set had shown. Nor, as he discovered, were the furniture designers he approached. It was only when he contacted architects of what he called the 'modern' school that his demand for a cabinet which satisfied both the functional task of accommodating the radio technology and being 'attractive and saleable' were met.

Wyborn first approached Raymond McGrath (whose design was not produced) and Serge Chermayeff, whose design, the AC64, went on the market in 1933. This increased sales 100 per cent from the previous season.[34] The experiment proven, Wyborn next invited Coates to provide designs for the 1934–5 season. His proposal for a circular cabinet – the AD65 – was as simple as it was radical, and was a brilliant response to the process of manufacture. As Jeffrey Meikle has noted, everything about a circular design made production easier: the mould was easier to produce, it facilitated the flow of molten resin during the moulding process, was easier to remove from the machine and more easily polished. Its rounded form was more durable as it had fewer corners or points to be knocked.[35] And just as he had done at Lawn Road, Coates used the structure to determine the motif of the design. The casing became a series of variations on the circle: at the centre was a circular speaker grille, above was placed the station band in a semicircle, while below were the round tuning and volume knobs. Available in either brown or black Bakelite (the latter with chrome fittings), or in brighter colours to order, the basic set cost just over £8 (with hire purchase available). It sold exceptionally

top: **Publicity shot for the AD65 wireless at the Radiolympia Exhibition, 1934**
above left: **Publicity shot for the AD65 wireless – here with its specially designed stand – at the Radiolympia Exhibition, 1934**
above right: **AD65 wireless for Ekco, 1934**

top: **Coates with the design team at Ekco, 1947**
above right: **Princess Wireless set for Ekco, 1948**
above left: **Radiotime Wireless set for Ekco, 1947**

well – 40,000 sets in six months – increasing Ekco's sales by 25 per cent.[36] Versions of the design continued to be made throughout the 1930s, and it went into production again after the war. In what was clearly a happy relationship, Coates would work with the company as a consultant until the early 1950s, designing casing for the new Thermovent heater when Ekco expanded into domestic products in 1937, and producing the Princess 'handbag' set and Radiotime clock radio, as well as a television, between 1946 and 1948.

That Ekco was a pioneer of modern manufacturing techniques was recognised in the most significant contemporary account of industrial progress, Nikolaus Pevsner's 1937 *An Enquiry into Industrial Art in England*, in which he famously declared that 90 per cent of British goods (though not Ekco's) were without aesthetic merit. While Pevsner was a little disappointed to discover that three quarters of the sales of the AD65 were for brown sets (because, as Wyborn noted, it matched the furniture better; it also cost £2 less than the black-and-chrome version), he noted that the combination of the Chermayeff- and Coates-designed sets had meant that the company's turnover increased from £200,000 in 1930 to £1.25 million in 1936. Moreover, Pevsner argued that Ekco exemplified the way forward for British manufacturing, as it had realised 'that to get something really new and convincing one has to go to the best men', and that these men [sic] should be architects. Such patronage resulted, as Adrian Forty has noted, in the rather curious fact that the work of the most avant-garde designers of the day, hitherto unknown outside a metropolitan elite, was brought directly into people's homes.[37]

Work for the BBC

It seems probable that Wyborn had found his 'best men' in Chermayeff, Coates and McGrath, because of their involvement in the design of the interiors of the new Broadcasting House in London for the BBC, which was completed in the summer of 1932. Like Ekco, the BBC represented the emergence of a form of patronage that designers such as Coates saw as integral to the realisation of a modern British design culture. Although not a state body, the corporation's monopoly over the provision of such a potentially subversive medium as broadcasting was based on the notion that it would operate for the public good, and edify as much as it entertained. For many of those who worked there this command of the airwaves represented an unprecedented opportunity to bring high culture to the public through its programmes, hence the commissioning of talks from poets like T. S. Eliot and writers such as Virginia Woolf. Similarly, when the corporation outgrew its premises at Savoy Hill, the commissioning of a new headquarters building offered the chance to support the emerging generation of British modernist architects, an act of advocacy similar to that of another contemporary monopoly, the Underground Group in London led by Frank Pick. As part of the agreement over the purchase of the site (from a developer with a hotel scheme killed by the economic downturn), the commission for the building itself had gone to Val Myer, an architect whose design was firmly in what would now be called an Art Deco style.

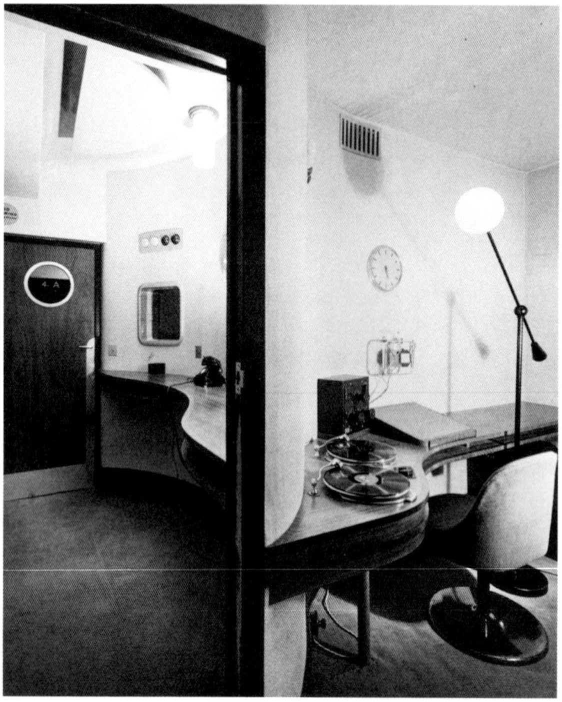

The interiors were, however, to be designed separately, on the basis of the widely held belief 'that the broadcaster's surroundings must affect his performance; that a gay dance band should have a gay room, that plays and sketches should be produced in studios resembling a theatre'.[38]

The chief protagonists in bringing modernist designers to the BBC were its Assistant Commissioner, Valentine Goldsmith, and the producer and pioneer of sound broadcasting, Lance Sieveking. The latter was a close friend of the painter Paul Nash, and part of London's bohemian set. Goldsmith was active in the DIA.[39] Their first recruit was Raymond McGrath. His work at Finella, the house at Cambridge which he had recently transformed into a modernist salon-cum-home, with rooms designed around particular narrative themes using the latest materials and technology, made him eminently suitable, they thought, for overseeing the variety of interiors to be incorporated into Broadcasting House. He was duly appointed Decoration Consultant. Serge Chermayeff, who had recently finished the interior of the Cambridge Theatre in London, was approached separately to join him, as was Coates, who had come to Goldsmith's attention on the recommendation of Paul Nash.[40] The men would be nicknamed 'The Three Musketeers' by the editor-proprietor of the *Architectural Review*, H. de Cronin Hastings, for whom the commission represented a significant stamp of (nearly) public approval for the new architecture.

above: **News Studio at Broadcasting House, London, 1932**

On the basis of his experience as a designer of commercial spaces, and his background in engineering, Coates was given the most technical studios to design: those for special effects, for mixing sound and for news broadcasting. The challenge he faced was considerable. Like all the designers he not only had to work with the BBC's engineers to accommodate soundproofing technology, then in its infancy, but, in a period when no standardised broadcasting equipment existed, he had to invent the tools which would facilitate the new medium of wireless broadcasting. This encompassed not just obvious things like a microphone and gramophone decks, but also chairs, sound-effects machinery and the dramatic control panel through which the sounds produced in the studios floors below were mixed into the final broadcast.

In the news studios, for example, Coates created a setting in which the newsreader could function effectively and, crucially, quietly. Thus, he designed the combined gramophone and reading desk and its chair to support actively the process of broadcasting. The chair was designed to swivel horizontally, and to fit neatly into the return of the desk. This allowed the broadcaster to sit as close as possible to the small desk lectern and, in one movement with the chair, turn silently to attend to the gramophone turntable to the left. In addition, as a further means to limit unnecessary movement, the custom-made microphone was designed like a shaving mirror and could be pulled nearer to the speaker as necessary.

above: **Dramatic Effects Studio, Broadcasting House, 1932**

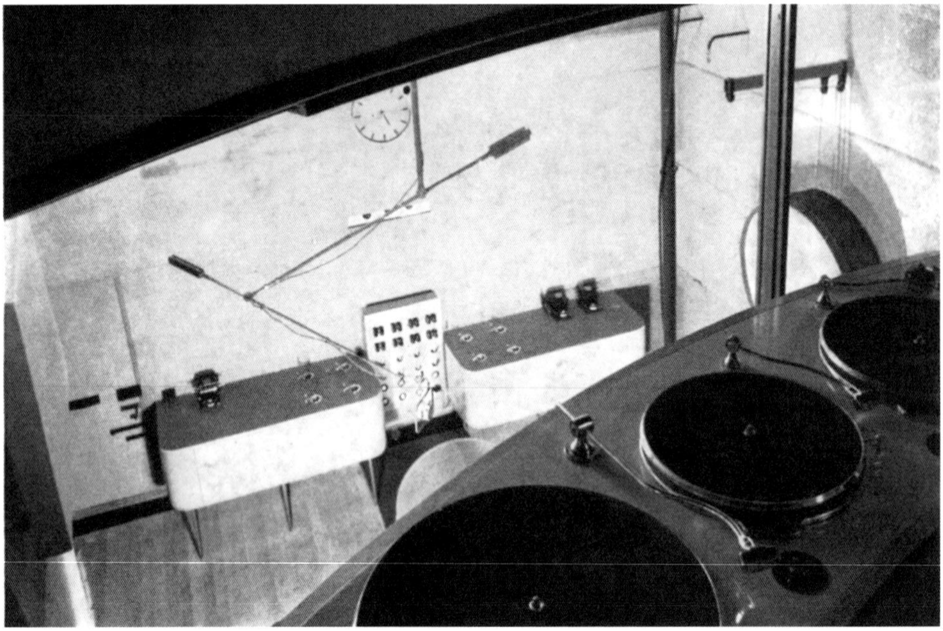

Coates applied similar design principles in the gramophone-effects studios, which occupied two stacked volumes within the double-height space of the main Dramatic Effects studio on the sixth floor (an arrangement which presaged the Yeoman's Row interior). Here, the bank of six turntables formed the top of a curvilinear cabinet which contained felted shelves to hold the records. From the windows of these studios the operatives could see into the main effects room, for which Coates designed a wind-machine cage, a central effects table which could rotate, and an electrical-effects bench, among other devices.

The general consensus among contemporaries was that the interiors, unlike the exterior, were a triumph, and, in the words of F. E. Towndrow, editor of *Building*, 'a great step forward to the new architecture of scientific humanism'.[41] Coates's designs were singled out as the best. Gerald Wellesley declared them 'alive, brave and new',[42] while Robert Byron recognised the motive underlying the commission in his judgement that 'Mr Coates's rooms and their fittings are the finest in the building and they show what the phrase "design in industry" could mean if an introduction were effected between Mr Coates and a few industrialists.'[43]

As the call from Ekco shows, the BBC work did indeed bring about such introductions. It also brought Coates commissions from the gramophone manufacturer EMG, and a further job from the BBC to design its new studios in Newcastle upon Tyne

above: **View of the gramophone decks and down into the main space of the Dramatic Effects Studio, Broadcasting House, 1932**
previous page: **Dramatic Control Room, Broadcasting House, 1932**

(completed 1935). The BBC would also work for Coates. For, several times over the next 20 years, he would be invited to broadcast his own Modernism from its studios, starting with the 1933 discussion with Geoffrey Boumphrey on the modern dwelling. This access to the most up-to-date form of media would prove vital to Coates's mission to propagandise Modernism, not just through his architecture but also through the written word and collective action.

If Coates's identification with Wyndham Lewis's persona of the artist-intellectual had not already predisposed him to leadership of the emerging body of card-carrying Modernists in England, his intellectual background, and his desire to theorise his practice, made it almost inevitable that he should take the lead in transforming what, in 1930, was a rather disparate group of individuals, into a tight-knit avant-garde by 1933. It should, however, be remembered that until he met Pritchard, Coates knew hardly any architects, establishment or otherwise. Maxwell (Max) Fry (1899–1987) was not yet a convert to the cause, and Coates's aesthetic modernity was still shaped by his association with the painters and bohemians of Fitzrovia. It was Pritchard who gave him the entry point into the (albeit small) world of those interested in the modernisation of architectural culture when he took him to Finella, whose interiors had been constructed almost entirely from Venesta products.

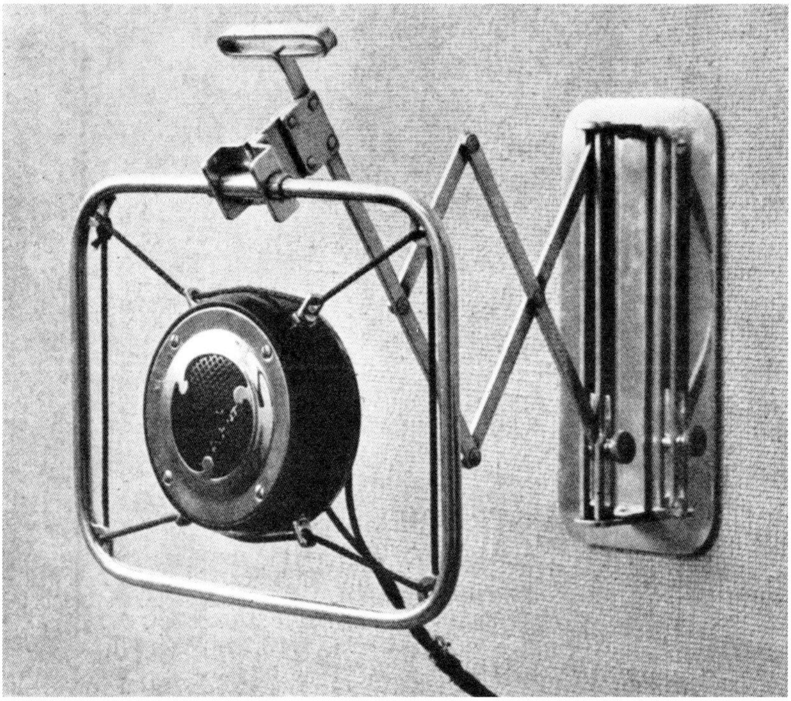

above: **The custom-designed microphone for the News Studio at Broadcasting House, 1932**

Propagandising Modernism: Towards the MARS Group

At Finella, its patron, the Cambridge don Mansfield Forbes was already taking the first steps towards the institutionalisation of Modernism, and in the summer of 1930 he announced his plans to create a company to produce modern architectural designs. In another sign of his ruthlessness when the opportunity arose to effect change, Coates saw his chance, and by the September had hijacked Forbes's plans and established the Twentieth Century Group (TCG). In Coates's mind, its chief purpose, given the as yet inchoate nature of the British Modern Movement, was 'to define the principles to which contemporary design should conform',[44] and next 'to put across Modernismus in England', through the means of an exhibition of modern design on the model of those recently held in Stockholm, France and Germany.[45] He was, however, overambitious. The group's membership was too diverse to achieve anything, comprising as it did hard-core Modernists like Pritchard and Coates and, a new ally, Chermayeff (another Finella *habitué*), alongside the much more genteel Noel Carrington of the DIA and *Country Life* books; Howard Robertson, Head of the Architectural Association; and Forbes and McGrath. It argued itself out of existence within two years.

The same period saw Coates, again with Pritchard, but now joined by his old friend Max Fry, who had finally pledged himself to the cause, attempt to infiltrate the DIA and win it round to modernist design principles. This effort was more successful. Pritchard and Fry served on the DIA committee while Coates worked on the 1933 Exhibition of British Industrial Art in the Home, for which the Association was partly responsible.[46] This, as noted above, featured the full-scale mock-up of the Lawn Road minimum flat: valuable publicity for both Isokon and Modernism as a whole, not least because it stood alongside a model Week-end House designed by Chermayeff.

The DIA, like the TCG, was, however, a group too catholic in its tastes to provide more than a resting place for Coates and his co-conspirators. Although they had provided valuable experience in committee and exhibition work, they lacked a purely architectural focus, and Coates was increasingly impatient to bring together those he had identified as suitably like-minded in order to work to reform architectural culture. The autumn of 1932 was to prove a crucial turning point in the achievement of this aim. First, around this time, he joined with Paul Nash in discussions about the formation of a small group dedicated to the promotion of Modernism across the arts. After a very careful process of membership selection, this became Unit One, announced to the press in June 1933 as standing for 'the expression of a truly contemporary spirit, for that thing which is recognized as peculiarly *of to-day* in painting, sculpture and architecture'.[47] This idea of a small cell (11 members in all), wedded to a particular aesthetic principle, and working through exhibitions and writing to advocate their point of view, was the final lesson Coates could draw on in the wake of the receipt of another fateful letter, this time from Sigfried Giedion, Secretary of CIAM (the *Congrès Internationaux d'Architecture Moderne*) hoping to find a British contingent suitable to become national representatives:

top: Coates at a CIRPAC meeting, Amsterdam Municipal Museum, 1935, Le Corbusier is seated at the left of the table
above: Coates and Verner Moser at a CIRPAC meeting, Amsterdam, 1935

> Please let us know if interest in the new architecture is still so lukewarm in England, and whether there are really no young men to be found there who have the courage, and feel it is their duty, to form a collective organisation, and establish contact with us.[48]

Giedion had written the letter at the suggestion of P. Morton Shand, a key pro-modernist contributor to the *Architectural Review*, the journal in which Coates's work at 1KPG had been published the previous July. Coates felt able to reply in the affirmative, and on 28 February 1933 the MARS (Modern Architectural Research) Group (the name was Coates's invention) was founded as the British branch of CIAM.[49]

Under Coates's direction, MARS was formed as an architectural avant-garde, one which through a small core membership would inveigle itself into institutions and discourses through strategic alliances and the infiltration of the contemporary media. The founding members were all connected to Coates, and numbered his partner David Pleydell-Bouverie and Fry, as well as three media contacts: Morton Shand, de Cronin Hastings and John Gloag, the part-time journalist and member of the DIA who also worked for the advertising agency Pritchard, Wood and Partners (owned by Jack Pritchard's brother Fleetwood). Although the membership would expand to include, among others, F. R. S. Yorke, and Amyas Connell, Basil Ward and Colin Lucas, as well as Lubetkin, and the assorted members of Tecton, it was always carefully vetted (Coates would name Joseph Emberton, Howard Robertson, Grey Wornum, Oliver Hill, Wamsley Lewis and Oswald Milne as architects of the type he would exclude from joining should they apply for membership, on the grounds that their collective identification with 'the cause' was insufficient and their architecture too stylistically diverse).[50]

The MARS Group pursued two core activities. As part of CIAM, it was required to research and design prototype solutions to contemporary problems, for presentation at congresses and other meetings. So within weeks of formation, members were hard at work developing hypothetical plans for a slum-clearance scheme in Bethnal Green, east London. This activity took Coates into the heartland of European Modernism, and by July 1933 he was on board the SS *Patris*, as the British delegate to CIAM IV. There he met Le Corbusier, with whom he remained friends for the rest of his life. In 1935, his status as the leading British Modernist was recognised in his appointment to CIRPAC, CIAM's central organising group.

At home, MARS's work was to change the present and future of architecture. Thus, much care was taken to engage the emerging generation of students with modernist ideals by serving on crits, giving talks in schools and providing placements for students in their offices, as Coates would do. More broadly, the group sought, in Fry's words, to persuade 'the talkative individuals of the day' – the architectural profession, policy makers and so forth – of the relevance of the new architecture to the resolution of the problems of the day.[51] Typical of this approach was its collaboration with the reformist Housing Centre throughout the 1930s. The alliance would prove an invaluable one, for, by wartime, the Centre had become a respected voice in reconstruction debates. The main element of this association would be a series of contributions to the Centre's own

displays at the biennial Building Trades Exhibition at Olympia. These offered a critique of, and alternatives to, current planning orthodoxies and offered a valuable platform for MARS to engage with the profession.

Its first contribution was to the Centre's 1934 show, at which were displayed the plans for Bethnal Green.[52] In a sign of the group's concern to move the architect's persona away from that of the individualist practitioner, the work was presented as that of a group of anonymous technicians – undoubtedly a Coatesian conceit designed to signal the architect's expert status. In order that the work should reach the audience of architecture and building professionals who could not make it to Olympia, immense care was taken to ensure the display was reported copiously in the press. Reports in the *Architects' Journal*, *Design for Today* and *Town and Country Planning* duly followed.

A similar strategy was pursued when, after much discussion, the group finally held its own exhibition, 'New Architecture, an exhibition of the elements of modern architecture', in January 1938. Held at the New Burlington Galleries, London, its message was reinforced by several pages of coverage in the March 1938 issue of the *Architectural Review*. The group then took a version of the show to the 1938 Building Trades Exhibition. Although Coates contributed to the March exhibition, and remained a committed member of MARS, his involvement in CIRPAC kept him away from the day-to-day activity of the group that he had founded.

above: **CIAM members posing for Ernö Goldfinger at the Temple of Poseida at Sunium during the CIAM IV conference in 1933. Left to right: Mancha Sert, Ricardo Ribas, Wells Coates, José Torres Clavé and José Luis Sert**

By the end of the 1930s, Coates had succeeded in establishing himself, *ex nihilo*, as an architect, created the foundations on which a British Modern Movement rested and launched himself on the international scene. The approach of war, however, led, as it did for all his contemporaries, to a decline in commissions, and not long after hostilities had commenced Coates closed his office and returned to uniform.

Notes

1 Jack Pritchard, lecture on Isokon, 1973. JPA PP/14/4/2.

2 Coates to Jack Pritchard, letter, 17 January 1930, WCA Box 23.

3 The original scheme is illustrated in C. G. Holme and S. B. Wainwright, *Decorative Art, 1930, The Studio Year Book*, London, The Studio, 1930, p.58.

4 'Dr Rosemary Pritchard's Speech' at the opening of Lawn Road Flats, July 1934, JPA, PP/16/2/23/3.

5 Jack Pritchard to Lord Pentland, letter 18 October 1930, JPA, PP/15/1/11/3/2.

6 Memorandum of March 1932, cited in C. Buckley, *Isokon Exhibition*, Newcastle, University of Newcastle, 1980, p.2.

7 Correspondence between Isokon's solicitor and the Board of Trade, 31 December 1931 and 8 January 1932, JPA, PP/15/3/1 and PP/15/3/1/4.

8 Jack Pritchard, *View from a Long Chair, the Memoirs of Jack Pritchard*, London, Routledge & Kegan Paul, 1984, p.79.

9 Further Isokon flat ventures were mooted – to the designs of Walter Gropius and Maxwell Fry – at Birmingham, Manchester and at St Leonard's Hill, but were never built. The latter is featured in F. R. S. Yorke and Frederick Gibberd, *The Modern Flat*, London, The Architectural Press, 1937, p.13.

10 Molly Pritchard, memorandum, 7 September 1930, WCA Box 25.

11 Wells Coates, 'Furniture Today, Furniture Tomorrow – Leaves from a Meta-Technical Notebook', *Architectural Review*, July 1932, p.32.

12 Count Herman Keyserling, *The Travel Diary of a Philosopher*, London, Jonathan Cape Ltd, 1925 (2 vols; translated by J. Holroyd Reece), pp.180–1.

13 My thanks to John Allan, architect for the renovation of the flats, for his comments on the planning of Lawn Road, interview July 2008.

14 Letter from Jack Pritchard in *Private Eye*, no. 636, 2 May 1986, p.12.

15 The Isobar took on this role when it replaced the

above: **Le Corbusier's visit to the MARS exhibition, 1938. Left to right: Godfrey Samuel, Le Corbusier, Wells Coates, J. M. Richards, Serge Chermayeff, Maxwell Fry**

14 Letter from Jack Pritchard in *Private Eye*, no. 636, 2 May 1986, p.12.
15 The Isobar took on this role when it replaced the kitchen space on the ground floor.
16 'Dr Rosemary Pritchard's speech', July 1934, JPA, PP/16/2/23/3/1.
17 Gerald Barry, *News Chronicle*, 12 July 1934, clipping in JPA, PP/16/2/23/4/4.
18 'Modern Dwellings for Modern Needs', *Listener*, 24 May 1933, pp.819–21.
19 For which, see the *Architects' Journal*, 20 July 1933, p.65.
20 Brochure for Embassy Court, n.d. (c.1936), WCA Box 4.
21 Yorke and Gibberd, *The Modern Flat*, p.72.
22 C. H. Reilly, 'The Year's Work at Home', *Architects' Journal*, 16 January 1935, p.109.
23 'Pull down the Front', *Argus*, 16 February 1935. My thanks to Kes Dron for this clipping.
24 Wells Coates, 'Planning in Section', *Architectural Review*, August 1937, pp.51–8. Subsequent quotations are from this text until signalled otherwise.
25 'The "Three-two" Planning System', *Architectural Review*, April 1939, p.178.
26 Wells Coates, Notes for a Lecture to the Reiman School, 14 June 1939, WCA, No 6. The Reiman School was a well-known private design school, the talk was to students attached to Duncan Millen's Department of Interior Design.
27 Randal Bell describes this encounter and their subsequent collaboration in Laura Cohn (ed.), *Wells Coates, Architect and Designer 1895–1958*, Oxford, Oxford Polytechnic Press, 1979, pp.65–8.
28 Nicholas Stephen, 'Palace Gate Flats, London', *Building*, July 1939, p.282.
29 'Sunspan House, Olympia', *Architects' Journal*, 26 April 1934, p.610.
30 *Daily Mail* Ideal Home Exhibition catalogue, 1934, p.111.
31 'Sunspan House, Olympia', *Architects' Journal*, p.610.
32 Houses survive in Hinchley Wood, Long Ditton and Coombe (Surrey), and at Angmering, Chadwell St Mary, Essex and Havant.
33 John Wyborn interviewed in Walter Landauer, 'Plastics', *Trend in Design in Everyday Things*, 1, (1936), pp.82–3. All quotations are taken from this until signalled otherwise.
34 Nikolaus Pevsner, *An Enquiry into Industrial Art in England*, Cambridge, Cambridge University Press, 1937, pp.105–6.
35 J. Meikle, 'New Materials and Technologies' in C. Benton et al., *Art Deco, 1920–1939*, London, V&A Publications, 2006, p.355.
36 Tom Going, 'E. K. Cole Ltd.', unpublished paper, June 1990, Southend Museum Archives.
37 Adrian Forty, 'Wireless Style', *Architectural Association Quarterly*, spring 1972, p.30.
38 Sydney A. Mosley, *Broadcasting in my Time*, London, Rich and Cowan, 1935, p.48.
39 Richard S. Lambert, *Ariel And All His Quality, An Impression Of The BBC From Within*, London, Victor Gollancz, 1940, p.168.
40 Valentine Goldsmith to Coates, letter, 28 October 1930, WCA Box 7/C.
41 F. E. Towndrow, 'Current Architecture', *Building*, July 1932, p.402.
42 Gerald Wellesley, 'The Decoration of the Studios' in *The BBC Yearbook*, London, BBC, 1932, p.115.
43 Robert Byron, 'Broadcasting House', *Architectural Review*, 72, August 1932, p.49.
44 'Agenda for [TCG] meeting at Arts Club, Dover Street, 26.2.31', WCA Box 12/D.
45 Mansfield Forbes to Lance Sieveking, letter, 9 September 1930, Sieveking Papers, Lilly Library, Indiana University, Bloomington, Indiana. See also 'Brief Statement of the Twentieth Century Group', *c.*September 1930, reproduced in Serge Chermayeff and R. Plunz (ed.), *Design and the Public Good, Selected Writings 1930-1980 by Serge Chermayeff*, Cambridge, Mass., MIT Press, 1982, pp.109–10.
46 Noel Carrington, *Industrial Design in Britain*, London, George Allen and Unwin, 1976, chapter 11.
47 'A New Group of Artists', *The Times*, 12 June 1933, p.10.
48 Sigfried Giedion's letter to Coates, cited in A. Jackson, *The Politics of Architecture*, London, Architectural Press, 1970, p.34.
49 'Confidential memorandum, 28 February 1933, The INTERNATIONAL CONGRESS OF MODERN ARCHITECTURE' [*sic*], WCA Box 12/A.
50 'Memorandum of 1 March 1933'. WCA Box 12/A.
51 Max Fry, 'How Modern Architecture came to England', Pidgeon audio-visual set, *c*. 1980.
52 On this, see J. Ledeboer, 'New Homes for Old', *Design for Today*, 2 (1934), pp.407–8.

4 An Architecture of Our Times

In a wartime letter to his daughter Laura, Coates described with optimism his hopes for the future: 'I have always thought that there was much work to do: but now perhaps after the war, we of the modern architectural school can say perhaps we will have a real chance to do it, without old men's nonsense interfering. So we can work for peace, for better homes and conditions for the people.'[1] The election of a Labour government in summer 1945, committed to the creation of a new society, and an architecture to match, must have affirmed this view.

Four years later, Coates's optimism was faltering and he lamented that despite his status as a 'pioneer in the modern scene' and being 'at the height of [his] powers as a planner, thinker and designer', other Modernists, 'some of them even trained in one's own office', were gaining public appointments over him.[2] Even a short-lived partnership with the town planner Jacqueline Tyrwhitt could not win him the opportunity to design a New Town.

Coates attributed the lack of commissions to his absence from London during the war, and claimed that the 'old gang' of the RIBA had prevented him from gaining another significant post-war commission, the design of the BBC's new studio complex at White City, west London. This went to Graham Dawbarn, who, Coates cattily remarked, 'has never even seen a TV set.'[3] Active service had not, however, prevented many of his modernist contemporaries and their successors from winning commissions. Rather, the dogmatism and single-minded determination to disrupt the British architectural scene including, necessarily, the RIBA, which had so powered Coates in the 1930s, and done so much to establish Modernism's post-war hegemony, was out of place in a world where commissions lay in the hands of politicians who, however progressive, required more diplomacy and humility from their architects than he could muster. Nevertheless, until his early death in June 1958, Coates did sustain a practice, producing a range of work as inventive and ambitious as his pre-war designs, though much of it went unrealised, and which cemented the legacy which has continued into the present. His concern to maximise the use of new technologies and materials, and through them to create environments which equipped people to function effectively in the modern world, remained unchanged. His wartime experience, however, provided both a new set of influences on these themes, and the potential to put them into practice.

opposite: **Wells Coates, 1947**

From War to Peace

A member of the RAF Reserve, Coates was called up in November 1939. Initially appointed to the Air Staff in London as a Technical Staff Officer, by 1942 he had been transferred to the Ministry of Aircraft Production, during which time he was based mainly in Bristol. In both settings, his role was to work on the design of fighter aircraft, including the De Havilland Vampire jet, in recognition of which he was appointed a military OBE in January 1944. One outcome of this activity was his subsequent commission from De Havilland's to design the cabin layout and fittings for a special version of its Dove aircraft, completed in 1946. Such commissions, alongside his existing work for Ekco and EMG, cemented his reputation as an industrial designer. In 1944 he was appointed Royal Designer for Industry by the Royal Society of Arts, and became the master of its faculty between 1951 and 1953. Indeed, Coates was much in demand as a teacher of design, not least from the reorganised Royal College of Art, but he declined these offers in the expectation of work in what he always considered his primary sphere of activity, architecture.

In this respect, the most significant part of his wartime RAF service was his secondment, during 1944, to the Aircraft Industries' Research Organisation on Housing (AIROH). As thoughts turned to reconstruction in 1942, members of the aluminium industry, whose entire production was then geared to wartime needs, realised that

above: **Interior of De Havilland Dove Aircraft, 1946**

they needed to anticipate the end of this market and make plans for the realities of peacetime. This coincided with the beginning of government plans for a programme of emergency housing in the immediate aftermath of peace, whenever that should come. AIROH was formed in the same year to investigate ways of using the methods, and materials, of aircraft production to produce what one its founders, W. Greville Collins, called 'a completely factory-made house which could be built on an assembly line'.[4] After an initial prototype proved that the aircraft factory could 'productionise' house manufacture, the organisation was given the go-ahead by Stafford Cripps, then head of the Ministry of Aircraft Production (and in whose Bristol constituency a major aircraft factory was sited), to produce an aluminium-alloy prototype. To assist in the development of this, AIROH appointed a technical and design committee, and it seems likely that it was to this that Coates was appointed.

Although it was agreed that the plan and basic form of what became known as the 'aluminium bungalow' should conform to the main government prototype for emergency housing, the Portal bungalow, Coates and the team presided over a number of key innovations which made their design the only one of the four types of prefabricated houses ('prefabs') constructed under the Temporary Housing Act of 1944 to be genuinely prefabricated and built in the factory – an achievement which Coates later claimed for himself.[5] Each house would be made up of four sections of aluminium frame-and-panel

above: **One section of an AIROH aluminium bungalow being swung onto the lorry which will take it to the building site**

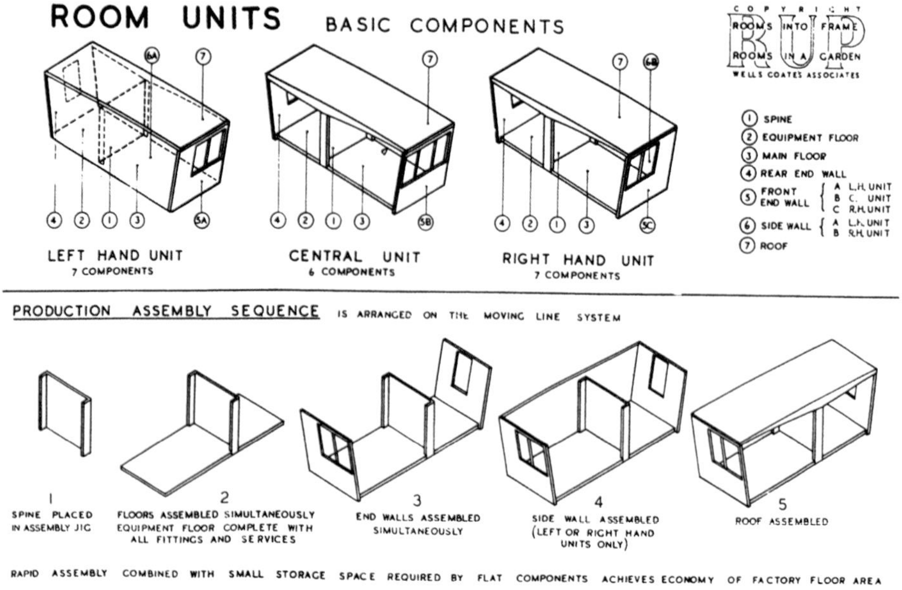

construction, insulated, and faced internally with plasterboard. All plumbing and wiring was done in the factory, and the bathroom-kitchen unit likewise pre-installed. Rattling off the production line at the rate of one per 12 minutes, the units were transported to site by lorry (whose dimensions determined those of each section – 7 metres long, 2.2 metres wide [23 feet by 7 feet]), whereupon they could be assembled by unskilled labour since they required only bolting to a ready-built dwarf wall. Of the 156,623 prefabs built after the war, 54,500 would be to the AIROH design.[6] So, just as he had done before the war with the design of the AD65 and its variants for Ekco (see Chapter Three), and as he had hoped in that letter of 1942, Coates played a significant role in bringing the benefits of a highly developed piece of technology to the lives of the many.

It was, no doubt, the apparent willingness of government to support technological innovations that encouraged Coates to use his AIROH experience as the basis for the reinvigoration of his pre-war plans for house types. Outlining his new scheme to Jack Pritchard in a letter of October 1947, he reminded his former collaborator that he had 'always been interested in methods whereby variant plans of houses … could be produced, with standardised methods of construction … to meet all forms of demand'. Reflecting that the Sunspan bungalow at Mardley Hill had, perhaps, been 'the first truly conceived piece of prefabrication in this country', he attributed its lack of correct replication to the fact that industry was not yet ready to take up prefabrication in 'the true sense'.[7]

above: **Diagram of the Room Unit concept**

top: **Model to demonstrate the Rooms in a Frame concept**
above: **Watercolour presentation drawing for Rooms in a Frame scheme for the St Lawrence Hotel, Ramsgate, 1946**

In anticipation of a transformed building industry, Coates developed a new dwelling system, named Room Unit Production (RUP), which combined elements of the Isotype and Sunspan methods of construction and the spatial planning concepts which underpinned the 3-2 system, with the material and production innovations of wartime aircraft manufacture. First worked through in 1945–6, when he proposed it for inclusion in the section devoted to designs 'not too far ahead of current manufacturing possibilities' at the 'Britain Can Make It' exhibition, it went through various iterations well into the mid-1950s.[8]

In a piece of breathless prose, surely derived from Richard Buckminster Fuller, whose influence can be seen in the conceptualisation of the system, Coates thus announced RUP as:

> A highly integrated system of producing under factory-controlled mass-production conditions, self-contained, fully-equipped, fully-serviced, fully-finished, self-supporting and transportable ROOM UNITS in variation to meet all forms of needs for accommodation.[9]

To be used for either emergency or permanent housing, the system revolved around a basic dwelling unit formed from three mass-produced frame-and-panel sections. These would be made from another of Coates's inventions – insulated structural laminates – layers of various materials (paper or fabric, light alloy, cast steel, reinforced concrete or welded aluminium) laminated under low pressure. All equipment would be built into the individual chassis, and the complete units then delivered to site to be assembled; again, the goal was to realise his vision of bringing the mechanised home to the mass market.

Materials aside, this scheme had much in common with the AIROH bungalow; where it began to differ was in the way in which Coates envisaged its use. He proposed two main categories of RUP: 'Rooms in a Garden' and 'Rooms in a Frame'. The former were individual house units available in various permutations according to the buyers'

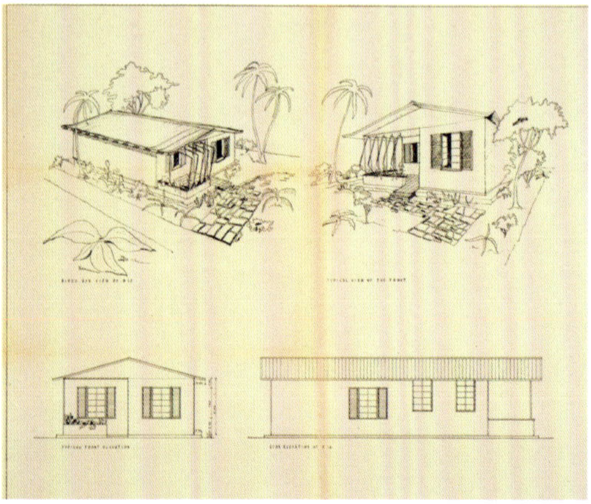

above: **Sketch of 'native housing' designed for South Africa, late 1940s**

needs: a couple might start with the basic single unit of bed-dressing room and bathroom plus kitchen-dining unit, and then add to it as their family grew with the nursery-playroom unit and so forth (step-and-staircase, and link and panel units were also available if buyers wanted to build upwards, or subdivide space). If this flexibility were not enough, and in keeping with his concept of the mobility of modern life, Coates envisaged that the 'Rooms in a Garden' should themselves be transportable: located in the city during the week, and then taken by lorry to sites in the country at weekends.

'Rooms in a Frame' was Coates's scheme for multistorey dwellings, comprising all types of the units slotted into a prepared framework. He thought it would be equally suitable for housing, hotels or hostels, and he did succeed in interesting a company, Hotel and General Catering Consultants Ltd, in commissioning him to design an extension to the St Lawrence Cliff Hotel, near Ramsgate, on this model in 1946. It was never built, although Coates did make alterations to the existing hotel on the site. In fact, no permutation of RUP would be realised despite the backing that Coates won for the scheme from manufacturers such as De La Rue plastics and the aircraft company A. W. Hawksley Ltd, for whom he worked on plans for RUP's application in the South American market and for what was described as 'native' housing for South Africa.[10] It was the retainers that these companies paid him which sustained his business in the immediate post-war years. However, in hindsight it might be noted that the considerable energy Coates spent on this concept, writing endless patent applications and proposals to potential sponsors, and endlessly refining the design, might have been better spent developing cordial relations with politicians rather than allying himself with the private industry which was still so subject to state control.

The Festival of Britain and the Telekinema

Even though Coates may have felt himself to have been overlooked by government in the years after 1945, there was one state-backed event in which, however many feathers he might have ruffled, it would have been unthinkable not to include him: the Festival of Britain. A nationwide event, it had as its centrepiece the site on London's South Bank where, in a country in which plans for reconstruction were, by and large, still at drawing-board stage, citizens could see for the first time the modernist forms which the post-war world would take. Given Coates's central role in conceiving this modern Britain, his participation was surely a certainty, but it was likely assured because decisions about the designers to be commissioned rested in the hands of a team of architects, most of whom were members of the MARS Group. Moreover, the whole event had been largely conceived, and was overseen, by Gerald Barry, who, in 1934, had declared Lawn Road to be the signpost to the new order now writ large on London's South Bank.

Coates was commissioned to design the interior of the Royal Pavilion (its exterior was designed by Michael Grice of Architects' Co-Partnership) and, appropriately enough, given his pre-eminence in the industrial design of modern communica-

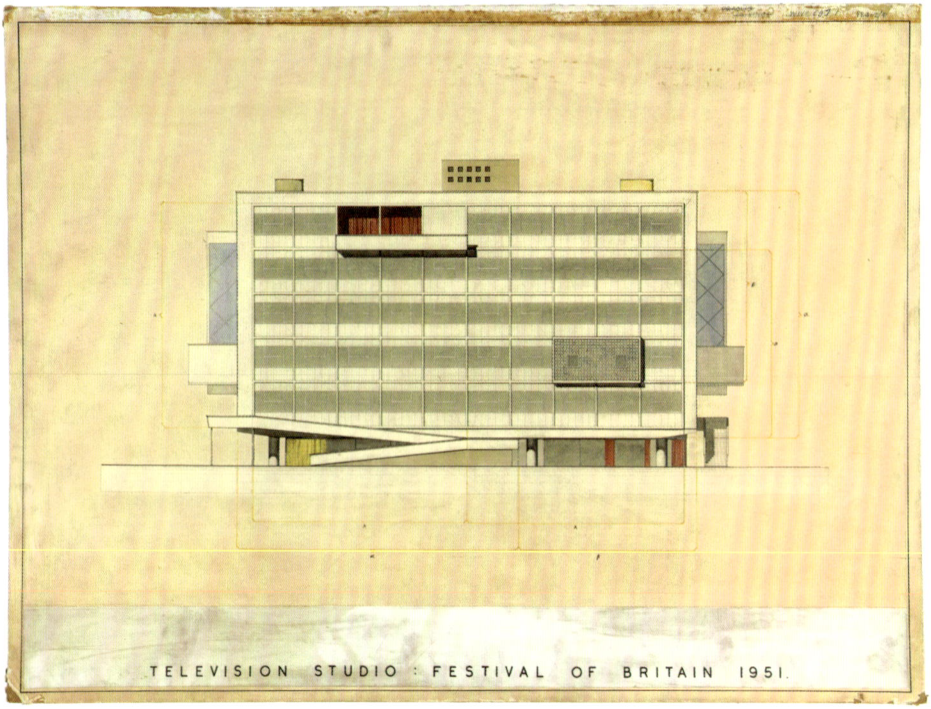

top: Elevation of the TV studio for the Festival of Britain, 1949
above: The Telekinema, at the rear of the piazza, and the Television Pavilion (right)

tions technology, a studio for the BBC, for which plans were abandoned in 1949; the Television Pavilion, which housed a display exploring television as a 'a new medium of entertainment'; and the Telekinema, 'the first cinema in the world to be specially designed and built for the showing of both films and television'.[11] The innovative nature of the brief suited Coates's design ethos and, as he had done so often before, he conceived the project, as he later explained, 'as a kind of laboratory experiment', one which, he added, he hoped would succeed, but should it fail 'it will have been in good spirit and in a gay mood'.[12]

In approaching the scheme, Coates had three main problems to resolve. First, the site was an awkward one, hemmed in between the railway viaduct to the Hungerford Bridge over the Thames, and the roundabout approach to Waterloo Bridge. Although this produced a roughly triangular plot, it was not sufficiently large to accommodate the usual fan-shape of a cinema auditorium. Thus the plan had to be for a parallel-sided building, with the entrance to the south. The site was also a very noisy one, so Coates had to produce a design which could dull the vibrations and echoes of railway and motor traffic on either side. Finally, the fact that the cinema would show both film and television either required two screens, or a means to accommodate two sorts of projector, and at the same time provide the sufficient throw to the screen and not reduce the accommodation, which was set at 400 seats. This was just the sort of puzzle-solving at which Coates excelled.

The completed building was as deft, and intellectually satisfying, as any of his pre-war designs. Structurally, it comprised two main sections: a block which housed the screen, auditorium and projection room; and an access block, containing the entrance, main staircase and the usual offices. The latter block, which was closest to the railway bridge, was structurally disconnected from the other by a 2.5 cm (1 inch) insulation gap, in order that it could vibrate independently and therefore not transmit vibrations through to the auditorium. The main block was formed from 25 cm (10 inch) thick reinforced concrete and insulated against noise and vibrations by what Coates described as an exterior-fixed 'quilt' comprising a series of insulating membranes of rockwool, cement render, and air space; the other side of the main wall was then faced with a further layer of rockwool, an air space and then an acoustic wall of fibrous plaster. Approved by the Building Research Station, the technique seems to have done the job and allowed the audience to watch the programme in peace.

In Coates's view, the novelty of the Telekinema lay in its sectional planning. The trick here was to work out how, within one space, to accommodate the shorter throw of the television projector without interfering with that of the film projection. One technological innovation was on his side, however, in reaching a design. The cinema would use 35 mm safety stock which was non-flammable, and thus removed the need, for safety reasons, to house the projection room above the audience. Another factor was that the ground level of the plot would, when the festival site as a whole had been terraced, sit three metres below that level. Both these conditions helped Coates move towards his eventual solution, which he called the 'lobster-claw section'. Since the immovable point

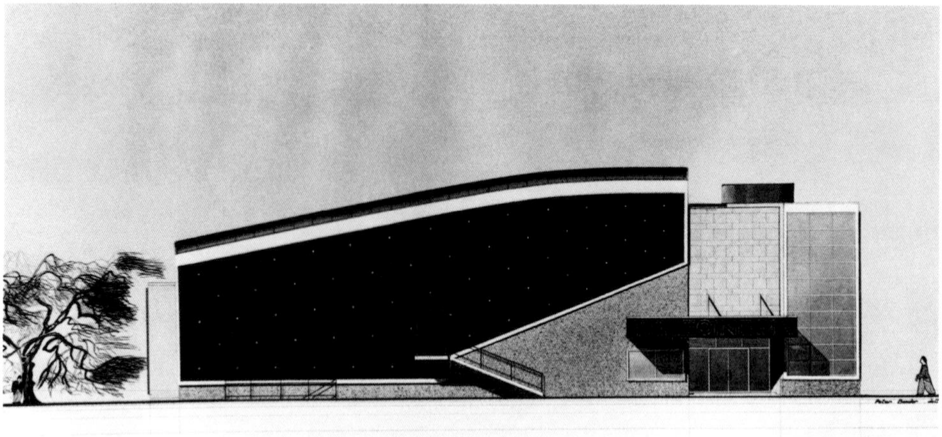

for the design was the throw of the television projector, Coates started the section with the screen and then marked back the requisite 14 metres (46 feet), siting the projection box at that point, in the centre of the section, producing a zero-degree projection level. The difference in throw between the two projection systems was accommodated by placing the projectors on tracks, along which they could be moved forward and back as needed. The contrast in levels allowed Coates to site a balcony level of seats on the box's 'roof' and, in the 'basement' level, place the stalls. Thus the projection room and its equipment became, as Coates wrote, the 'tidy morsel' gripped in the two arms of the lobster's claw.

With this fundamental problem resolved, Coates could attend to the delights of the design. Realising that the back of the projection room would face the audience as they entered the building, Coates decided to make a feature of its technology, which was considerable: the cinema not only combined dual methods of projection, but also pioneered the use of stereophonic sound and three-dimensional viewing. He therefore glazed in the box's rear wall to create a full-scale version of the perspex-encased wireless at Yeoman's Row. On the wall above, he invited his old friend John Armstrong to paint a mural which depicted the life of a film set. The blue-and-grey upholstery of the seats, designed by Coates, was by Lucienne Day, a colour scheme complemented by mahogany woodwork and bronze metalwork. The main feature of the exterior was, in an echo of the revealed technology of the projector room, the quilted insulating wall, rendered brown, of the auditorium.

The 'unpretentious, neatly designed little Telekinema', as the *Architectural Review* put it, was one of the few buildings, besides the Royal Festival Hall, to escape the cull of structures when the festival closed in October 1951.[13] Redecorated and fitted out as a

above: **Presentation drawing of the Telekinema for the Festival of Britain, South Bank site, 1951**

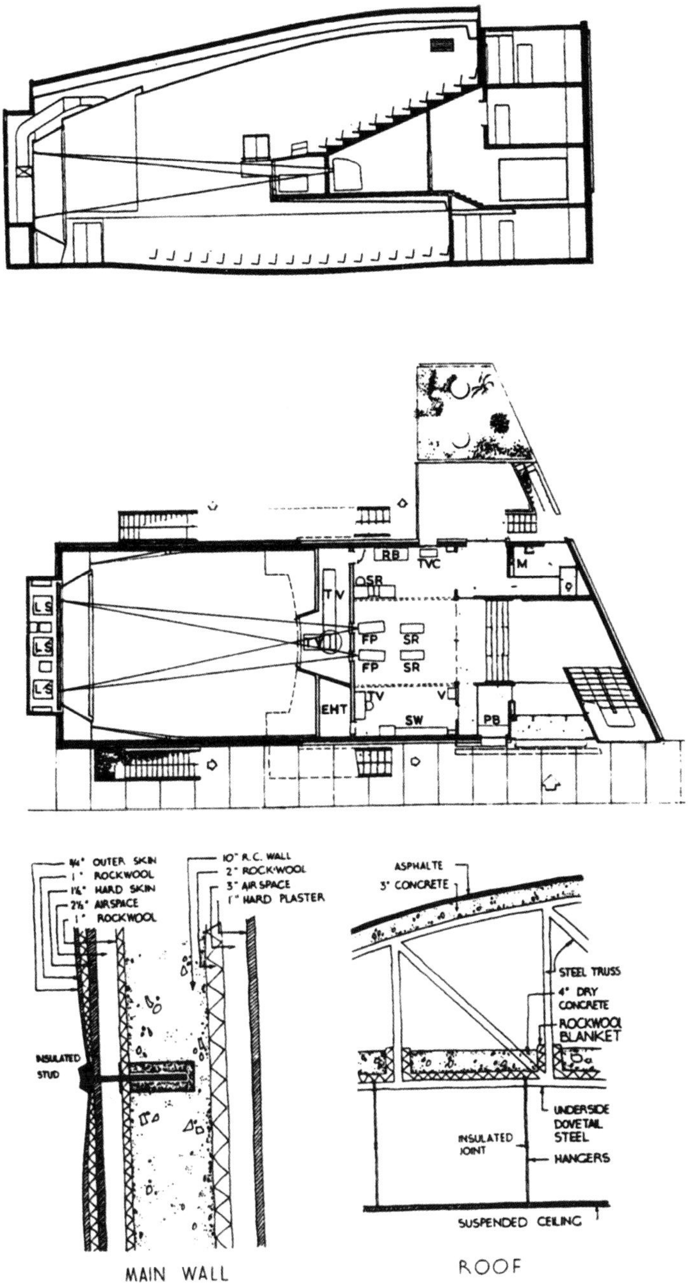

above: 'Lobster-claw' section, plan and soundproofing details of the Telekinema

top: **Telekinema auditorium**

above: **Mural design for the rear wall of the projection box by John Armstrong, 1951**

continuously operating film cinema, it became the home of the new state cultural body, the British Film Institute, and opened in October 1952. It lasted until 1957. For Coates, the prototypical nature of the design and its successful realisation led to another frenzy of attempts to promote it as the future form of the cinema. While he received many expressions of interest, and the cinema-industry press featured the design widely, again his ambitions were not realised.

The New Canada

Although Coates and his office produced a number of small schemes in the early 1950s – exhibition stands for firms such as Hawksleys, an interior for the Fashion Industries Club and a house at West Wittering, West Sussex – it became increasingly apparent to him that he might be better off looking overseas for the work and recognition he craved, and which he felt was his due. This realisation offered him the opportunity for a reinvention of self akin to that he had effected in the mid-1920s. Leaving the day-to-day running of the practice with his assistant, Michael Lyell, Coates shifted his purview, and his identity, to his 'native' Canada, and sought to recast himself as a guiding figure in the creation of the architectural setting for that country's emergence as a modern Commonwealth nation.

The new Canada would be founded on the exploitation of the country's rich stocks of mineral deposits, timber and grain. In British Columbia, which became Coates's main arena of activity, there was a fivefold growth in manufacturing between 1941 and 1961, with a commensurate demand for the business infrastructure to support such activity in city centres, and the housing to accommodate the workers whose labour powered this economic boom.[14] The free-enterprise politics of the province's governor meant that much of the new development was privately led, a condition which perhaps added further promise to Coates's change of direction, given his long experience of collaboration and invention with private enterprise.

An early indication of Coates's attitude to the development of a Canadian practice may be found in a letter to the vice-President of the Aluminium Company of Canada, which, like so many other similar concerns at this time, was developing plans for a new company town, in this instance at Kitimat, British Columbia. With Tyrwhitt, and a local architect, C. B. K. van Norman, Coates first approached the company in mid-1951 with proposals for a masterplan. When the commission went to a New York practice, Coates was not discouraged and instead proposed an alternative. Noting that the company had indicated that the architectural work would be given to a Canadian practice, he argued that it might consider the appointment of a consulting architect who would oversee the work of a team designing the different sectors of the new city, on the model used at Chandigarh, India.

Coates would, of course, take the Le Corbusier role, a post for which, he argued, he was suited on two grounds. First, because he was Canadian, and here he included a genealogical account of his family's national authenticity, and his own service in the

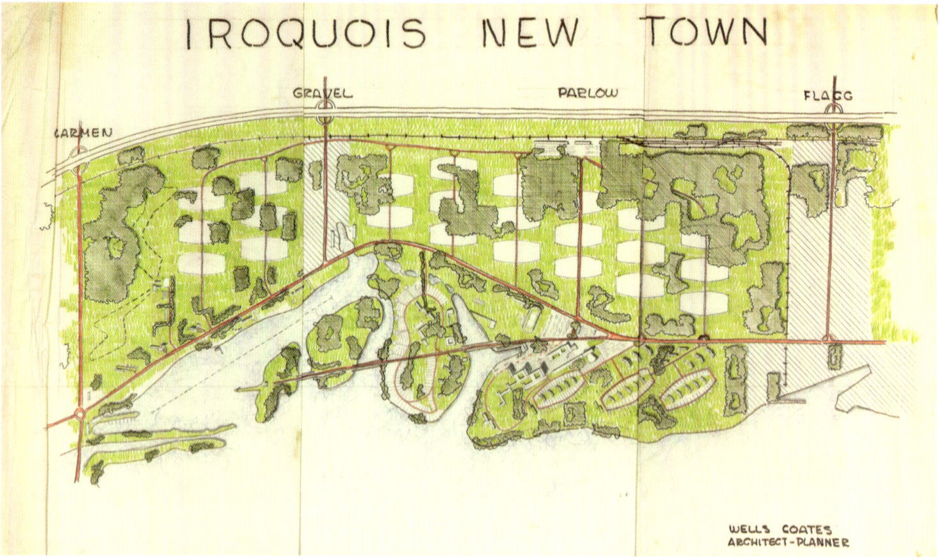

Canadian forces in the First World War. It is interesting that he now made no mention of the Japanese experience which had been so crucial to his self-fashioning since the late 1920s. Second, owing to his long service in the cause of the Modern Movement: 'I have', he declaimed, 'devoted the whole of my life towards training myself in the best tradition of contemporary architecture.' He also noted his considerable experience, thanks to his 'various official capacities' of 'handling groups of architects in a co-ordinated scheme'.[15]

The bid was unsuccessful, but it did not put Coates off, and he next turned his attention to a recently announced plan for the rebuilding of the town of Iroquois, Ontario. This was to be flooded as part of the plans to create the St Lawrence Seaway, and after lobbying local politicians he was appointed Planning Consultant to the municipal council to produce a masterplan for the town which would replace it. As Sherban Cantacuzino recounts, the project was for a small-scale relocation of the existing community. But Coates could not resist reworking the scheme into one for a new town, on the British model, which was intended to attract a new wave of British immigrants to Canada. Included in the new scheme was a factory to produce the room units and associated technology with which the residential areas of the city would be built. Coates spent two years assembling a syndicate, headed by his old friend Randal Bell, to fund and develop the scheme, but it came to nothing. The provincial government handed redevelopment powers to a major public utility company which had no use for such a scheme, and the masterplan design went instead to the Canadian architect, Kent Baker.[16]

A number of similarly grandiose projects followed: plans with developers for high-rise versions of 'Rooms in a Frame' in Ottawa and Vancouver; a scheme to redevelop Toronto Island; and plans for a monorail mass-transit system for the British

above: **Sketch Plan for proposed New Town at Iroquois, Ontario, *c.* 1952**

Columbia Electric Company. None succeeded. Why? It was at once Coates's greatest strength and disadvantage that he had the skill and grit to conceive and work through a project, invariably ingenious, intended to make a genuine contribution to the progress of society. At the same time, the very determination which enabled him to work on an idea too quickly became a dogmatism which refused compromise or did not know when to stop. His total immersion in the cause of architecture, attributable to his Damascene discovery of the discipline in 1927, also dulled his political sensibilities. So while such dogmatism might have been central to the successful promotion of Modernism in the 1930s, it played less well in both post-war Britain and Canada. His failure to understand the nuances of local politics surely hampered his ability to do business in British Columbia. A further miscalculation, originating, perhaps, in his disbelief that a pioneer such as he should have difficulties in finding work, was his assumption that there was a need for a guiding figure in the modernisation of the Canadian architectural scene. In fact, Modernism was already well established there, both in architectural schools and in practice, and although Canadian architects happily worked with him, he was, arguably, less the mentor than the co-worker.[17]

The disappointments of the Kitimat, Iroquois and other schemes was mitigated a little in 1955 when, thanks to Coates's long-held association with CIAM, the combined influence of Walter Gropius and José Luis Sert at Harvard led to an invitation to teach in its Graduate Design School, first for three weeks in April 1955, and then for the subsequent academic year. Here he could exploit his pioneer status, not least by joining forces with his old friend, and fellow musketeer, Serge Chermayeff, who later recalled: 'Students everywhere admired him, many were genuinely fond of him.'[18]

It was, perhaps, the combination of the ego boost of a year's successful teaching at Harvard and his eternal optimism that led Coates to decide to settle permanently in Canada in July 1956. Initially occupied by the transit-system designs, as well as a scheme for a new sort of Canadian design school (the Centre for Advanced and Unified Studies in the Applied Arts), Coates's next project, his final one as it turned out, was collaborative. Working with a group of leading Vancouver Modernists, including Arthur Erickson and Peter Oberlander, an urban renewal scheme for downtown Vancouver was begun in autumn 1956. 'Project '58', specially geared to 'spotlight the responsible role of downtown business interests in Urban Renewal', was to be an outline redevelopment plan for presentation at an exhibition held during the British Columbia centennial year of 1958.[19] The group had already received some support and interest from local business people when the project ground to a halt. Not this time for political reasons, but because on 18 June 1958 Coates suffered a fatal heart attack while swimming off Vancouver beach.

This was a sad and abrupt ending to a life which had seen great success and great disappointment, and one which, perhaps, with Project '58 might well have been entering a new era. But it was a life which, both before and after the Second World War, produced some of the most imaginative, clever and intrinsically modern solutions to the century's problem of creating better homes and conditions for its people. Above all, and

this is where Coates's chief legacy lies, it was a life dedicated to the cause of architecture more generally. He himself recognised this when in a rather poignant speech, given at the graduation banquet at the University of British Columbia's architecture school, he summarised the course of his life and its guiding principle since the late 1920s:

> I believe that we set out, to set up a program, a strategy, and a method, and that we accomplished just that: we plotted the main courses for navigation, for an architecture of our times.[20]

Coates's role as the instigator of Modernism as a collective project in Britain cannot be overestimated. The formation of the MARS Group in 1933 provided a focus for progressive architectural activity in Britain. Over the next two decades it attracted to its membership successive waves of architects who, inspired by the work of Coates and his contemporaries, pledged themselves to the development of a new architecture. They, in turn, developed the nature and theory of the native movement such that British Modernism was a prime mover in the reconfiguration of modernist theory as it entered the post-war era.[21] Coates remained an active and enthusiastic member of CIAM in the 1940s and 1950s, and regularly attended its conferences. His preference for clearly expressed concrete forms suggests that he was a parent of the New Brutalism, whether in the hands of his former partner Denys Lasdun or in those of Alison and Peter Smithson, perhaps his true heirs, not least in their dogmatism and determination to shake up the British scene.[22]

The problem-solving and prototypical nature of his architecture meant that Coates was, perhaps, always an 'architect's architect', and it says something about the esteem in which he was held by his contemporaries that he received a number of notable and lengthy obituaries as well as a collective effort to memorialise his legacy.[23] Coates's death coincided with the end of CIAM and the consequent winding up of the MARS Group, whose members agreed that its residual funds should be put towards an exhibition of his work. Worked on variously by Max Fry, Jane Drew, Jack Pritchard

above: **Coates, with Alison Smithson and Paul Reilly behind him, at the 21st anniversary party for Lawn Road Flats, 1955**

and later Coates's daughter Laura, this eventually became a monograph by Sherban Cantacuzino published in 1978 and an exhibition, held in Oxford, in 1979.[24] The same year saw the reconstruction of the Lawn Road minimum flat for the Arts Council's epoch-celebrating exhibition, 'The Thirties'.

More recently, as this book began by noting, the years since 2000 have seen the renovation of the Lawn Road Flats, Embassy Court and parts of 10 Palace Gate. This process suggests not just the recognition of Coates's significance but more importantly the continued relevance of this insightful, inventive and passionate man's approach to the creation of environments which allow people to live, and live well.

Notes

1 Coates-Laura Coates, 9 June 1942, WCA Box 35.
2 Coates-J.M.Richards (also to Max Fry, Patricia Strauss and others), letter of 12 December 1949, WCA Box 30.
3 ibid.
4 W. Greville Collins, 'The "A.I.R.O.H." House' in John Madge (ed.) *Tomorrow's Houses. New Building Methods, Structures and Materials*, London, Pilot Press, 1946, p.207.
5 Coates to Jack Pritchard, letter, 25 October 1947, WCA Box 9.
6 Colin Davies, *The Prefabricated House*, London, Reaktion Books, 2005, p.63.
7 Coates to Jack Pritchard, letter, 25 October 1947, WCA Box 9.
8 Coates to Council of Industrial Design, 'Confidential Description of Project number 1', memorandum of 22 September 1946, WCA Box 9.
9 Wells Coates, 'Project Number One', proposal submitted to Council of Industrial Design, 11 September 1946, WCA Box 9.
10 Plans in WCA Box 9.
11 Ian Cox, *The South Bank Exhibition. A Guide to the Story it tells*, London, HMSO, 1951, p.83.
12 Wells Coates, 'Planning the Festival of Britain Telekinema', *British Kinematography*, vol. 18, no. 4, 1951, p.108. All references are from this article until signalled otherwise.
13 'The Exhibition as Landscape', *Architectural Review*, August 1951, p.128.
14 Rhodri Windsor Liscombe, *The New Spirit. Modern Architecture in Vancouver, 1938–1963*, Montreal, Canadian Centre for Architecture, 1997, p.45.
15 Coates to McNeely Dubose of ALCAN, 2 March 1952, WCA Box 9.
16 Sherban Cantacuzino, *Wells Coates, a monograph*, London, Gordon Fraser, 1978, pp.92–5. See also Elspeth Cowell, 'Wells Coates' Toronto Island Redevelopment Project', *Bulletin of the Society for the Study of Architecture in Canada*, vol. 20, no. 2, pp.41–50.
17 See Windsor Liscombe, *The New Spirit. Modern Architecture in Vancouver, 1938–1963* for an account of Canadian Modernism.
18 Serge Chermayeff to Sherban Cantacuzino, 1971, cited in Laura Cohn, *The Door to a Secret Room, a Portrait of Wells Coates*, Aldershot, Scolar Press, 1999, p.221.
19 'Project 58' brochure, WCA Box 9.
20 'Wells Coates 1895–1958', *Journal of the Royal Architectural Institute of Canada*, v. 36, June 1959, p.210.
21 See Eric Mumford, *The CIAM Discourse on Urbanism*, London and Cambridge, Mass., MIT Press, 2002, chapter 4.
22 As noted in Manfredo Tafuri and Francesco Dal Co, *Modern Architecture*, vol. 2, London, Faber and Faber/Electa, 1986, p.230.
23 See, *inter alia*, J. M. Richards's in the *Architectural Review*, December 1958, pp.357–60; *The Times*, 20 June 1959, p.13 with follow-on letters from Gordon Russell, 25 June 1958, p.13 and Patrick Heron, 16 July 1958, p.14; and Raymond McGrath in *RIBA Journal*, August 1958, p.357.
24 Cantacuzino, *Wells Coates, a monograph* and Laura Cohn (ed.) *Wells Coates, Architect and Designer 1895–1958*, Oxford, Oxford Polytechnic Press, 1979.

Afterword: Conserving Lawn Road and Embassy Court

However acclaimed the Lawn Road Flats and Embassy Court were on their completion, as the years went on, and especially as the buildings entered into their 'middle age', both began to encounter serious problems. At times, it seemed that both would face demolition or, at best, a life far removed from their clients' and designer's original intentions. The experimental nature of their construction was, in part, a factor in this downturn in fortune. It was also caused by complications over, and changes to, ownership, which resulted in the consistent neglect of the upkeep necessary to maintain any building to habitable standards, not least icons of Britain's Modern Movement. The fact that both blocks have now been rescued from neglect and restored as closely to their original condition as contemporary housing legislation allows reflects the coming together of residents, conservation professionals, architects and amenity societies in order to ensure that their significance was not left to be recorded only in history books, but remains intact and in vibrant three-dimensional form in Belsize Park and on the Brighton seafront.

The problems began for Lawn Road in the late 1960s. Seeking a way of freeing themselves from the responsibility for funding the maintenance of the block, Jack and Molly Pritchard began to explore the possibility of finding a new owner to replace them. After an approach to a hospital failed, in 1969 they accepted an offer from the *New Statesman and Nation* (which had absorbed the journal in which Gerald Barry had declared Lawn Road a signpost to a new order) in the belief that it would understand and maintain the building in its original spirit. As Jack wrote later, this belief turned out to be misguided and the purchase had largely been an investment on the journal's part; three years later, the block was sold to Camden Council for over twice the original price.[1]

Now part of the council's housing stock, the building slowly entered a period of decline. Keen to maintain the integrity of the block (in which he and Molly still lived), Jack negotiated with the Chair of the council's Housing Department, Corin Hughes-Stanton, himself a design journalist, to ensure that the domestic service was continued for existing tenants, and that the maintenance of the building was put under the aegis of its Architects' Department. Day-to-day management became the responsibility of the Housing Department. However as soon as Hughes-Stanton was no longer in post, the deal was not honoured. Thus, throughout the 1970s and 1980s, and in a period of increasing economic decline, the council struggled to combine responsibility for a work of architectural significance (a status recognised by its listing at Grade II in 1974) with

above: **Lawn Road Flats after renovations**

the economic practicalities of managing a block of flats which, by virtue of their small size, became increasingly hard to let.

The consequence was a series of unfortunate decisions, which began to destroy the original architectural and social quality of the block. Chief among these was the destruction of the Isobar and its kitchen, and their replacement with three flats, and, in 1984, the installation of a new heating system which resulted in external heating pipes standing out prominently on the building's rear façade. These were supposed to be temporary and were scheduled for removal in 1988, but financial crises in that decade meant that Camden was unable to replace them. By 1990, the physical deterioration of the building attracted the attention of the then newly founded conservation body Docomomo, which campaigns for the conservation of modernist architecture across the world. It convened a meeting at Lawn Road attended by conservation groups (including the Thirties Society, now the Twentieth Century Society) and residents, some of whom had considered buying the block from Camden, a move which marked the beginnings of concerted, albeit lengthy, attempts to restore the block to a state which recognised its historical significance.

above: **Lawn Road flats in disrepair in 2000**
opposite top: **Lawn Road in disrepair: the access balconies**
opposite: **Lawn Road in disrepair: flat interior**

Pressure from Docomomo, which had been trying to interest a housing association in the block, and from the Twentieth Century Society mounted. English Heritage placed the flats on its Buildings at Risk register and threatened enforcement action over the heating pipes. In 1994, Camden responded by commissioning Troughton McAslan (later John McAslan and Partners) to prepare a masterplan for the complete restoration of the building. Delivered in February 1995, this proposed four phases of work, of which only one, the refurbishment of one double flat as a 'show flat', and some external repairs, was completed in 1998, at a cost of £250,000.[2] The extrapolation of this cost to the whole block (some £2 million) led the council to consider, given its many other housing responsibilities, whether the money might be better spent elsewhere and, despite political scruples, whether the building should be sold.[3]

above: **Lawn Road in disrepair: damaged kitchen**

It was another two years before a decision was formally taken. In the meantime, the block was gradually emptied of its tenants and became victim to serial vandalism. A listing upgrade to Grade I in 1999 emphasised the need to find a solution based on strict conservation principles. The Twentieth Century Society renewed its campaign for action, arguing that its sale was the best solution, noting of the flats that 'their design and cachet makes them an excellent proposition for a private scheme for single professionals or commuters, for whom the architectural and historical cachet would be a draw. Marketing of the building in this direction is strongly recommended.' [4] At the same time, various social housing solutions were aired in the local press, and negotiations were also undertaken for the sale of the block to the Peabody Trust. Local residents' associations also sought to change the use of the block so that it could be converted to use as a hotel or residential club, but this proposal was refused in January 2000. Finally, in October 2000, the council decided to put the block on the open market, specifying that the complete restoration of the block would be a condition of sale. Among those shortlisted as serious bidders were the Architectural Association school, which wanted to turn the block into student accommodation, and the Groucho Club, which saw its potential as an apartment hotel. In the end, however, the council settled on a bid more thoroughly in keeping with the Pritchards' original objectives. In 2001, it was sold to a consortium of the Notting Hill Housing Trust, Avanti Architects and the Isokon Trust, formed by Chris Flannery, a local architect who had become increasingly appalled at the decline of the block. They pledged to spend £2 million on restoration and to split the refurbished accommodation, with 11 flats sold off on the open market (including the Pritchards' penthouse) and the rest sold on a shared-ownership basis to key workers in the borough. A contract was formally signed in January 2003, and the following month council approval was granted to Avanti's programme of work.

Three years later, the restoration was complete. Carried out with advice from, and the approval of, English Heritage and the Twentieth Century Society, the block remains more or less faithful to the original design, but with some subtle adaptations to modern space standards and materials. Double glazing was installed, while to save costs in refurbishing the kitchens, several centimetres were shaved off each dressing room's width in order that standard white goods could be installed. More substantial work was carried out on the structure of the building and the roof. The strength of the foundations, found to be only 50 centimetres (20 inches) deep and causing subsidence, was improved by enhancing the ground around them. The roof was replaced and internal partitions – originally comprising steel-mesh lathing suspended on wires (the Briacanion system), and which had almost completely collapsed by the time work began – were replaced by metal-stud plasterboard partitions, with improved acoustic qualities. The original layouts, however, were retained. Externally, after two months of grit blasting, the concrete finish was found to be in reasonable condition, though only 10 centimetres (4 inches) thick. Local repairs were effected and the original colour restored – a light pink – when a new layer of render

was applied. The internal faces of these walls, which originally comprised cork and then a layer of plaster, had mostly degraded, and were again removed and replaced with thermal laminate-board lining, thereby improving insulation values. Wherever possible, the original fitted furniture was reused, and original ironmongery likewise. On its completion in December 2004, the project was widely celebrated in the press as a model of the sensitive and imaginative restoration to life of a key 1930s building.[5]

A similar recovery from adversity can be found in the recent history of Embassy Court. What makes its story remarkable is that its restoration was driven by its residents, rather than, at least initally, an outraged community of architectural and conservation professionals. The residents' spirit of campaigning, in keeping with the

above: **Embassy Court in disrepair: main elevation**
opposite top: **Embassy Court in disrepair: rear balconies**
opposite: **Embassy Court in disrepair: rear access balcony**

77

decade in which the block was built, would surmount considerable obstacles. The flats' demise began somewhat later than Lawn Road's, Embassy Court retaining its reputation as a well-appointed block well into the 1970s. It was listed at Grade II (and upgraded to II* in 1998) in 1984 as part of the 'accelerated resurvey' ordered by the then Environment Secretary Michael Heseltine following the demolition of the Art Deco Firestone Factory in Brentford, west London. Around this time the block attracted the attention of developers and its freehold was sold and passed through the hands of several landlords. In consequence, general maintenance was not carried out and the building, always vulnerable to concrete decay because of its seafront location, became increasingly dilapidated and run down. In response, in the early 1990s a group of lessees began what was initially a campaign to force the freeholder to carry out maintenance. Fifteen years later, and following assorted attempts to find alternative uses for the block, in 2004, the lessees, now organised under the aegis of Bluestorm Ltd, ended up acquiring, via the Royal Courts of Justice, the freehold itself.

The pages of Brighton's local newspaper, the *Argus*, provide a detailed account of the lessees' attempts, and their struggle to find a freeholder who could balance the demands of a listed building of considerable significance with the maintenance and management of a large residential block.[6] As at Lawn Road, though this time unsuccessfully, attempts were made in the late 1990s to link the block with a housing association. But, dependent on both the success of bids to the government's Single Regeneration Budget and the Heritage Lottery Fund, and the need to buy the leasehold of over a quarter of the flats, this proposal came to nothing. It did, however, produce a feasibility study by Alan Phillips Architects, which found the building to be structurally sound, despite the dilapidation. This example of raised and then failed hopes characterised the next seven years. November 2001 saw the lessees hold a public seminar at the University of Brighton to discuss options for the block, at which Phillips proposed that the block be partially converted to a hotel in order to fund the restoration of the flats in the upper storeys, while Alan Powers of the Twentieth Century Society spoke on the architectural significance of the block. Again this came to nothing. It was not until the legal action was nearing resolution that Bluestorm was able, in August 2003, to commission architects to prepare a scheme for renovation. Work began the following year to the plans of Conran & Partners, the majority of the work funded by contributions from individual leaseholders: a testament to the 'hold' of the design, some 70 years after its completion.

As at Lawn Road, the intention of the project was to respect the original building, but the work was not as thoroughgoing as at Belsize Park. No work would be carried out to the interiors of individual flats, not least because the block remained inhabited throughout the restoration, with the exception of a new heating system (individual boilers) to replace the communal system embedded in the floor plate of each flat. The lifts were overhauled, and windows and doors were replaced to match the originals (long since lost), including the reinstatement of the splendid chrome entrance doors. The extensively cracked roof slab was repaired with a chemical inhibitor gel, which also

top: **Embassy Court entrance after renovations**
above: **Embassy Court today**

creates an impermeable barrier against further corrosion, while the concrete render was repaired and new render, including an anti-carbonation agent, applied.

The completion of the project during 2005–6 was marked with considerable joy in the city of Brighton and Hove, and with respect in the pages of the architectural press.[7] Today, the block maintains its restored dignity alongside the community spirit which led to its rebirth, with many of its residents actively promoting the history of the block through research and a regular programme of tours and events: a happy blend, which could usefully serve as a blueprint for the rehabilitation of other modernist masterpieces in the future.

Notes

1 Jack Pritchard, *View from a Long Chair, the Memoirs of Jack Pritchard*, London, Routledge & Kegan Paul, 1984, p.99.

2 'Isokon Flats, Lawn Road, Hampstead', *Architects' Journal*, 15 January 1998, p.49.

3 'Isokon Flats to be sold off to private developers', *Architects' Journal*, 8 October 1998, p.9.

4 Letter from Twentieth Century Society caseworker to Camden Council, 6 October 1998, Twentieth Century Society Lawn Road case file. Much of this text draws on a synopsis of these records prepared by Alan Powers.

5 See, for example, Jan-Carlos Kucharek, 'History Lessons', *RIBA Journal*, October 2005, pp.79–82 and Catherine Croft, 'Isokon', *Architects' Journal*, 30 June 2006, pp.25–37. For a useful synopsis of the work at Lawn Road, see also 'Isokon Flats Lawn Road Hampstead London NW3', information pack produced by Avanti Architects, 2004.

6 I draw primarily on the *Argus* for this account as well as the press pack issued by Bluestorm Ltd at the launch of the restoration programme in 2004, and on files in the offices of Conran & Partners, Brighton, for which thanks are due to Paul Zara.

7 See especially Kucharek, 'History Lessons'.

opposite: **Restored rear façade of Embassy Court**

WELLS COATES Ph.D. B.Sc.
ARCHITECT-ENGINEER
modern constructions · interiors · furniture

15, Guessens Court, WELWYN GARDEN CITY
HERTFORDSHIRE
PHONE · WELWYN GARDEN · 624

13th February, 1930.

Oliver Hill, Esq.,
9, Hanover Sq., London, W.1

Dear Sir * A friend of mine, Mr. Angus Davidson, secretary of the London Artists Association, happened to mention my name to Mr Ivon Hitchens, and the latter has written to me briefly about the "proposed new firm of decorative art" which you are establishing * Through some misunderstanding, Mr Hitchens thought I might be disposed to consider accepting the post of Business Manager of the proposed firm * I would not be prepared to do that, but I am certainly interested to hear of a new project organised on the lines suggested to me by Mr Hitchens, especially if it includes modern furniture and interiors, and it occurs to me that I might be of some service to you in the capacity of consultant: for instance, I would be prepared to undertake the work of drawing up plans, preparing estimates, and supervising the construction of interiors and furniture; or, I might be able to send you a selected range of actual furniture models, etc., for sale on commission through your organisation. In this connection I ought to add that I am now considering the question of setting up a small workshop near London for the construction of certain articles which I find it difficult to have made in England except under my supervision *

¶Perhaps I ought to say briefly that at an early age I learned to draw with a brush and to make things in wood with my hands, in Japan, where I was born * Someone has said: "The man whose eyes have been trained in the East can hardly bear to open them in the West,"-- and when I came "home" I believed it * My interests then naturally gravitated to science, engineering, and the study of modern materials, and since the war, I have been schooled in the "modern movement" to which I felt myself drawn for obvious reasons * I know personally most of the "modern" artists in England, and I also know something of the difficulties of combatting the anti-modern prejudices here:--difficulties which I believe are vanishing more rapidly than many people think * I should be glad to hear further news of your scheme *

Yours faithfully,

Wells Coates

List of Works

Although the Coates office kept meticulous records of each project it undertook, very little of this material has survived. There is, therefore, no definitive list of works with dates of commission or construction. The information presented here is compiled from all available sources and aims to be as inclusive as possible. The dates used refer to completion or, when this is unclear, the dates on which the project was published.

A single asterisk (*) indicates that it has been drastically altered, sometimes beyond recognition. A double asterisk (**) indicates that the project has been demolished. A triple asterisk indicates unexecuted projects (***). Asterisks in parenthesis represent assumptions in the absence of evidence.

1929

Shop for Crysėde Silks**

41 Green Street, Cambridge

Client: Alec Walker

Architect and Building News, 8 August 1930, pp.185–8

1930

Shop for Cresta Silks, 17 Westover Road, Bournemouth, Dorset**

Client: Tom Heron

Architectural Review, June 1933, p.261

Building, May 1931, pp.241–2

Shop for Cresta Silks, 92 Brompton Road, London**

Client: Tom Heron

Architectural Review, February 1931, pp.43–4

Factory for Cresta Silks**

25 Broadwater Road, Welwyn Garden City, Hertfordshire

Client: Tom Heron

The Cabinet Maker and Complete House-Furnisher, 3 January 1931, pp.17–18

Architectural Review, February 1931, pp.43–6

The Shoe and Leather Record, 13 February 1931, p.35

Building, May 1931, 241–2

Architectural Review, April 1932, p.163

1931

Shop for Cresta Silks, 155 High Street, Bromley, London**

Client: Tom Heron

Architectural Review, December 1931, opp. p.174; February 1932, p.77

Shop for Cresta Silks, 68 East Street, Brighton**

Client: Tom Heron

Architectural Review, December 1931, opp. p.174 & 175

Building, March 1932, pp.132–3

1931

Office**

33 Bedford Place, London

Client: Wells Coates

Architectural Review, February 1932, p.78

opposite: **Wells Coates letter, February 1930**

Venesta stand, Manchester

1931

Venesta Stand for the British Empire Trade Exhibition, Manchester**

Client: Venesta Ltd (J. C. Pritchard)
Architects' Journal, 29 April, 1931, p.126
Architectural Review, April 1931, p.148

1931

Venesta Stand for the British Empire Trade Exhibition, Buenos Aires**

Client: Venesta Ltd (J. C. Pritchard)
Architects' Journal, 31 January 1931, p.608
Architectural Review, June 1931, p.224

1932

House interiors**

1 Kensington Palace Gardens, London
Client: George Russell Strauss
Architectural Review, July 1932, pp.29–38
BBC, *Design in Modern Life*, London, 1933, pp. xiv–xv
Duncan Miller, *Interior Decorating*, London, 1937, pp.71–3

1932

News Studios, Dramatic-effects Studios, Gramophone-effects Studio, Dramatic Control Rooms**

Broadcasting House, Portland Place, London
Client: British Broadcasting Corporation
Architects' Journal, 25 May 1932, pp.689–93
Country Life, 28 May 1932, pp. 596–603
Architectural Review, August 1932, pp. 53–78
BBC, *Broadcasting House*, London, 1933, pp.41–44 and pp.54–55

Venesta stand, Buenos Aires

1932

Shop for Cresta Silks, 82a Baker Street, London**

Client: Tom Heron
Architectural Review, June 1933, p.261
Building, December 1932, p.555

Shop for Cresta Silks, 73 New Bond Street, London**

Client: Tom Heron

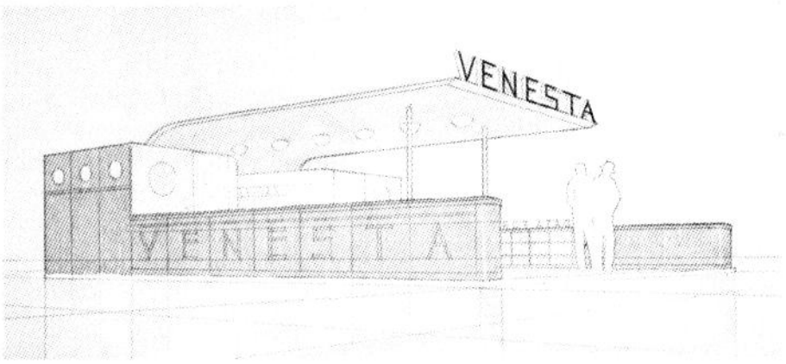

Venesta stand, London

1932

Office**

15 Elizabeth Street, London

Client: Wells Coates

Herbert Read (ed.) *Unit One*, London, 1934, p.106

1932

Venesta Stand for 1932 Building Trades Exhibition, Olympia, London**

Architectural Review, September 1933, p.116

1932

Design for an Airport***

(with David Pleydell-Bouverie)

Architectural Review, November 1932, p.201

1933

Bachelor Flat**

(with David Pleydell-Bouverie)

2 Devonshire Street, London

Client: Pryns Hopkins

Design for Today, May 1933, pp.12–13

Architects' Journal, 8 June 1933, pp. 755–57

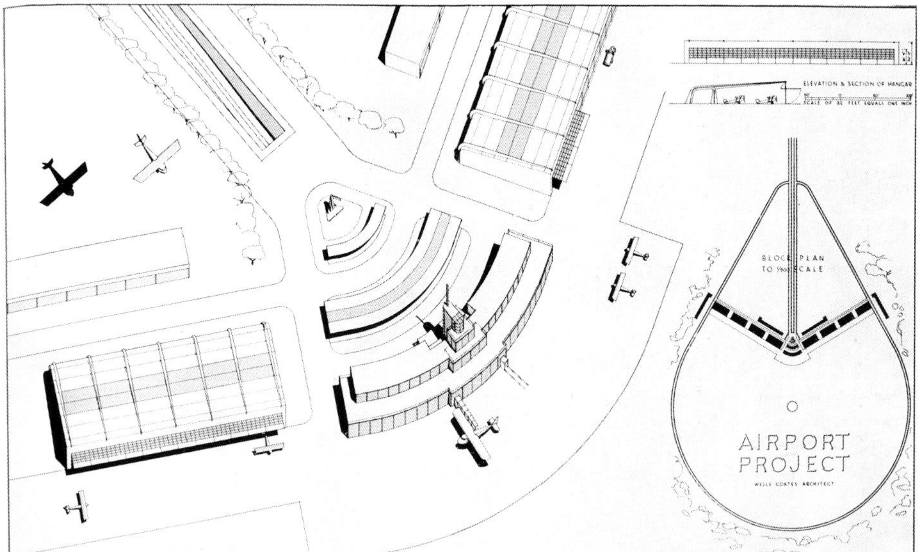

Design for an airport

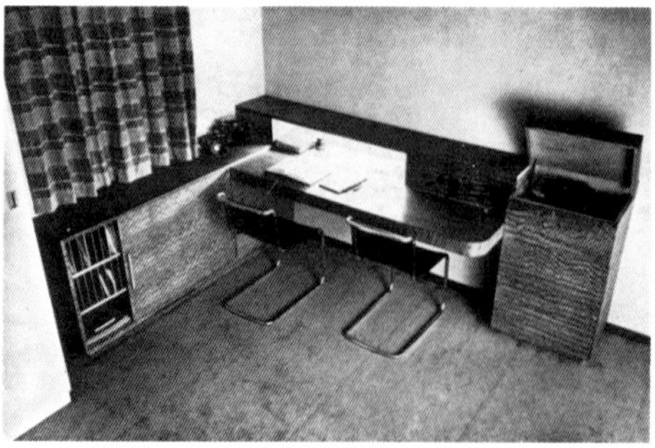

2, Devonshire Street

1933
Permanent Stage Set**
Old Vic Theatre, The Cut, London
Client: Lilian Baylis
Architect and Building News, 29 September 1933 (Architects' Portfolio 230)
Design for Today, May 1934, p.189

1933
Flat Interiors **
34 Gordon Square, London
Client: Elsa Lanchester and Charles Laughton
Woman's Journal, October 1938, pp.52–6

1933
A 'minimum' flat**
Exhibition of British Industrial Art in Relation to the Home, Dorland Hall, Lower Regent Street, London
Client: Isokon Ltd
Architects' Journal, 29 June 1933, pp.866–7
– 6 July 1933, p.14 and pp.18–19
Architectural Review, July 1933, p.25
– November 1933, p.199
– February 1934, p.43
Catalogue of The Exhibition of British Industrial Art in Relation to the Home, Dorland Hall, London, 1933, pp.19–21 (Coates also designed the National Gas Exhibit and Gas Kitchen)

1934
Second Feathers Club (with David Pleydell-Bouverie)**
Norland Gardens, London
Client: The Feathers Club Association
Architects' Journal, 1 March 1934, pp.318–319

1934
Sunspan house**
Daily Mail Ideal Home Exhibition, Olympia, London
Client: Associated Newspapers
Ideal Home Exhibition Catalogue, 1934, pp.111–12
Design for Today, April 1934, p.131
Architects' Journal, 26 April 1934, pp.607–9
The All-England Homefinder, May 1935

1934–36
Sunspan Houses*
E. & L. Berg Ltd
The only permanent example of the Sunspan House which used the intended constructional system houses is found at Mardley Hill, 1935 (see p.147). Berg built several one and two-storey versions of conventional construction at:
1 & 19 Avondale Road and 23 Southwood Gardens, Hinchley Wood, Surrey, 1934–5
1, 2, & 3 Wentworth Close, Long Ditton, Surrey, 1934–5
16, 57, 65 and 69 Woodlands Avenue and 25 & 70 High Drive, New Malden, Kingston-upon-Thames, 1934–5
Ideal Home, May 1934, p.334
There are also Sunspan houses built under separate contract by different contractors at: Sandy Lane, Chadwell St Mary, Essex (date unknown) Two storey versions: 47 Portsdown Hill, Havant, Hampshire, 1935
'Runnymede', Coastal Road, Angmering-on-Sea, West Sussex, 1936

Double flat at Lawn Road

1934
Lawn Road Flats
Lawn Road, London
Client: Jack and Molly Pritchard/Isokon Ltd
Listed: Grade I
Builder, 20 July, 1934, pp.92 and 106
Architectural Review, August 1934, pp.77–82
– September 1934, Plate IV 'The Model Kitchen'
Building, August 1934, pp.310–14
Architect and Building News, 10 August 1934, pp.154–8 and 'The Architect's Portfolio', no.264
Architects' Journal, 13 September 1934, pp.77–80
– 20 September 1934, 409–12
– 27 September 1934, 469–72
– 2 May 1934, pp.657, 674, 687, 690
Manchester Guardian, 3 January 1935, p.6
Decorative Art, Year-Book of the Studio, 1936, p.59 (colour picture and caption)
F. R. S. Yorke and F. Gibberd, *The Modern Flat*, London, 1937, pp.153–5
Catherine Croft, 'Isokon,' *Architects' Journal*, 30 June 2006, pp. 25–37

1935
Studio Flat**
18 Yeoman's Row, London
Client: Wells Coates
Architectural Review, November 1937, pp.51–8

1935
Entrance Hall, Porter's Box and Studios for the BBC**
54 New Bridge Street, Newcastle upon Tyne
Client: British Broadcasting Corporation
Architects' Journal, 28 February 1935, pp.329–31; 377–8
– 7 March 1935, pp.373–4
Architectural Review, February 1936, p.87

1935
Bungalow (Sunspan type)*
Lanercost Close, Mardley Hill, Welwyn Garden City, Hertfordshire
Client: Mrs M. H. Hill
Architectural Review, December 1936, pp.282–3
Ideal Home, May 1935, p.369
Alan Hastings (ed.) *Week-end Houses, Cottages and Bungalows*, London, 1939, p.100

Studio for the BBC, Newcastle

Sunspan Bungalow at Mardley Hill, 1935

1935
Embassy Court Flats
King's Parade, Brighton, East Sussex
Client: Maddox Properties Ltd
Listed: Grade II*
Architects' Journal, 23 August, pp.260–4, 271–2
– 30 August 1934, pp.203–4
– 14 November 1935, pp.741–6
– 23 January 1936, pp.161–2
– 30 January 1936, pp.201–2
– 13 February 1936, 271–2
Architectural Design and Construction, July 1935, pp.314–5
Architectural Review, November 1935, pp.167–73
Architecture Illustrated, November 1935, pp.143–8
Architect and Building News, 8 November 1935, pp.165–70 and 'The Architect's Portfolio', nos.318, 319, 320 and 321
Architectural Record, October 1936, pp.297–301
F. R. S. Yorke and F. Gibberd, *The Modern Flat*, London, 1937, pp.70–3
De 8 en opbouw, 17 July, 1937, pp.130–3
Jan-Carlos Kucharek, 'History Lessons,' *RIBA Journal* October 2005, pp. 79–82

1935
Ogmore School Camp* (with Elizabeth Denby)
Ogmore by Sea, Glamorgan, Wales
Client: National Council of Social Service

1936
Project for Flats, Ivor Court, Durdham Park, Bristol (with Denys Lasdun, revised by Edric Neel, 1937)***
Architectural Review, August 1937, p.51
Sherban Cantacuzino, *Wells Coates*, p.75, 195

1937
Shipwrights
Benfleet Road, Leigh-on-Sea, Essex
Client: John Wyborn

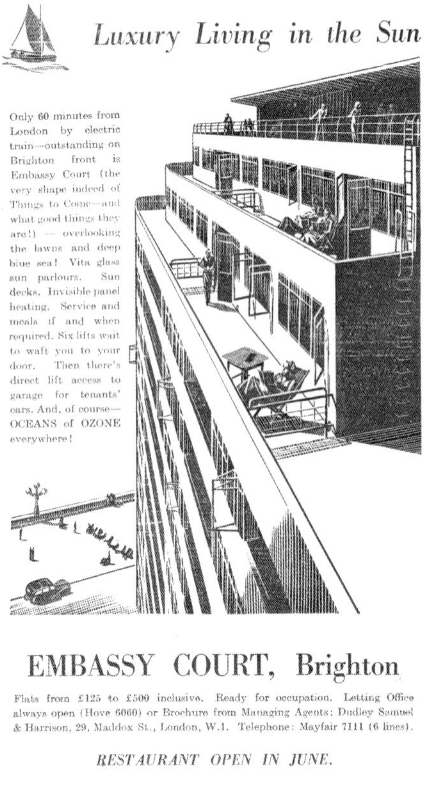

Advertisement for Embassy Court, 1936

1937
Shipwrights
Benfleet Road, Leigh-on-Sea, Essex
Client: John Wyborn
Listed Grade II*
Architects' Journal, 29 June 1939, pp.1121–2
The Ideal Home, October 1939, p.286
Alan Hastings (ed.) *Week-end Houses, Cottages and Bungalows*, London, 1939, pp.30–1
Ideal Home, September 1944, pp. 130–131

1937
Shop for Cresta Silks, 78 Brompton Road, London**
Client: Tom Heron
Architectural Design & Construction, May 1937, p.278

1937
Hampden Nursery School**
14 Holland Park, London
Client: George and Patricia Russell Strauss
Architectural Design & Construction, January 1938, p.38

Hampden Nursery School

1937
Hairdressing Shop, Canterbury (with Edric Neel)**
Client: L. E. Neel
Architectural Review, August 1937, pp.75–6

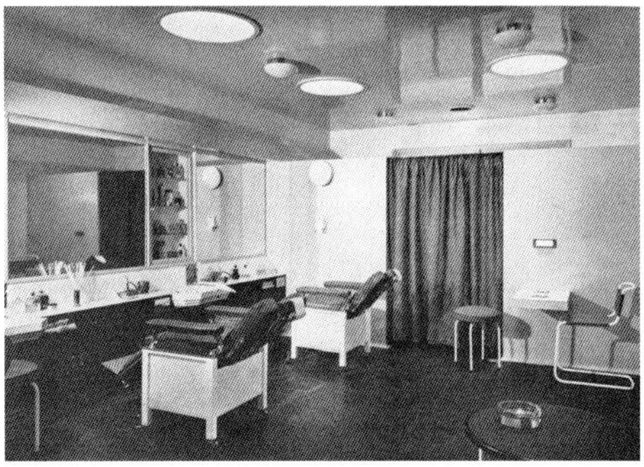

Hairdressing Shop, Canterbury

1937
News Chronicle Schools Competition (with Denys Lasdun and Associates)***
Architects' Journal, 25 March 1937, p. 530 and p.531

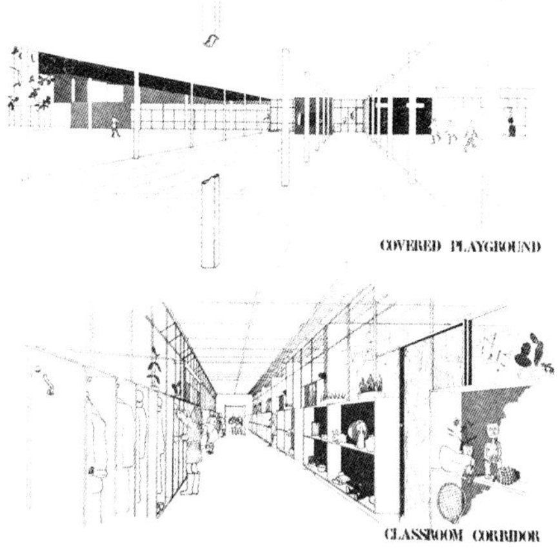

1937
'SCS' Slum Clearance project, Beaumont Estate, Stepney, London (with Denys Lasdun)***
Client: Randal Bell
Sherban Cantacuzino, *Wells Coates*, pp.75, 115
Laura Cohn, *Door to a Secret Room*, pp.196–7

Portsmouth Road, Esher, Surrey
Client: Commander A. L. Gwynne
Listed Grade II
Architectural Review, September 1939, pp.103–16
Ideal Home, June 1946, pp.21–32
Neil Bingham, 'The Homewood, Surrey', *Country Life*, 22 July 1999, pp.84–7
Neil Bingham, *The Homewood*, London, National Trust, 2004

1939
Palace Gate Flats
10 Palace Gate, London
Client: Ten Palace Gate Ltd (Randal Bell)
Listed Grade II*
Architectural Review, April 1939, pp.172–84
Building, July 1939, pp. 281–7
Architectural Record, November 1939, pp.34–9
Focus 2, 1938, p.65

1945–48
AIROH aluminium bungalow*
Built across England and Wales
Client: Ministry of Aircraft Production/Ministry of Health
Architectural Design & Construction, May 1945, p.115
RIBA Journal, July 1946, pp.402–5

1948
Interiors for the Fashion Industries Club, Brook St, London**
Client: The Fashion Industries Club

1948
Designs for Stands for Building Exhibition, Olympia, London**
Clients: A. W. Hawksley and Thomas French & Sons
Architects' Journal, 4 March 1948, pp.221–2

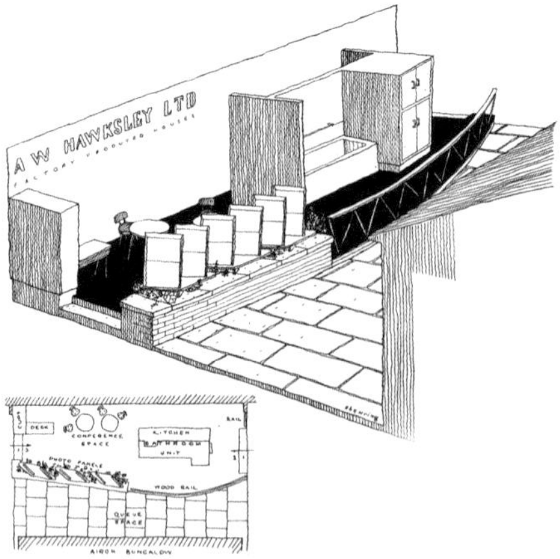

Hawkesley stand

1949
Stands for Building Exhibition, Olympia, London**
Client: James Clark and Eaton
Builder, 11 November 1949, p.627
Architects' Journal, 17 November 1949, p.551 – 1 December 1949, p.620
Architect and Building News, 25 November 1949, p.539

1951
Telekinema and Television Pavilion**
South Bank, London
Client: Festival of Britain
British Kinematograpy, April 1951, pp.108–19
Architects' Journal, 24 May 1951, pp.677–8
Builder, 6 July 1951, pp.11–13
Architectural Review, August 1951, p.94 and p.128
Ian Cox, *The South Bank Exhibition*, London, 1951, p.83
David Robinson, 'Film in 1951' in Elain Harwood and Alan Powers, eds., *Festival of Britain*, Twentieth Century Architecture 5, 2001, pp.88–94

Clark and Eaton stand

1952–53

Projects for Iroquois New Town***

Client: Iroquois Municipal Council/Randal Bell
Sherban Cantacuzino, *Wells Coates*, pp. 92–5
Elspeth Cowell, 'Wells Coates' Toronto Island Redevelopment Project', *Bulletin for the Society for the Study of Architecture in Canada*, vol.20, no.2, pp. 41–50

1955

Project for Flats, Ottowa***

Sherban Cantacuzino, Wells Coates, pp.72–3

1957

Project for Flats, Vancouver***

Sherban Cantacuzino, *Wells Coates*, p.74

1957

Toronto Island Redevelopment (with John Parkin)***

Cowell, 'Wells Coates' Toronto Island Redevelopment Project', pp.41–50

1957–8

House at West Wittering, West Sussex (with Michael Lyell)

Architectural Review, March 1958, pp.189–91
Ideal Home, May 1958, pp.42–3

1957–8

Mass Rapid Transit System***

British Columbia Electric Company
Laura Cohn, *Door to a Secret Room*, pp.188–191

1956–8

Project '58, Vancouver (with Arthur Erikson, Geoffrey Massey, Peter Oberlander and E. J. Watkins)***

The Canadian Architect, August 1957, pp.32–6

Industrial and Product Design (omitting fittings of buildings by Coates separately listed)

1928–29

Bow handles

Client: Taylor and Pearse Ltd

Unit Furniture, 1932

1932

Unit book boxes and Desk

Client: Isokon Ltd

Design for Today, May 1933, p. 31

Design for a gas fireplace(**)

Architects' Journal, 19 October 1932, p.503

Noel Carrington, *Design in the Home,* London, Country Life, 1932, p.105

Standard tubular steel furniture

Client: Hilmore and PEL Ltd

J. L. Martin and S. Speight, *The Flat Book,* London, William Heinemann, 1939, p.122

B. Campbell-Cole and T. Benton, eds. *Tubular Steel Furniture,* London, The Art Book Company, 1979

1934–1935

Wireless models AD65 (circular), AD36 (circular), AC85 (rectangular)

Client: E. K. Cole Ltd (Ekco)

Walter Landauer, 'Plastics', *Trend in Design in Everyday Things,* 1, (1936), pp.75–91

Nikolaus Pevsner, *An Inquiry into Industrial Art in Britain,* Cambridge, Cambridge University Press, 1937, pp.104–7

1933

Radiogram cabinets DR1, DR2 and DR3

Client: EMG Handmade Gramophones Ltd, with Davey Radio

J. L. Martin and S. Speight, *The Flat Book,* p.132

1934

Electric Radiant Fire

Client: J. C. Pritchard/Isokon Ltd

Collection University of East Anglia, Sainsbury Centre, Norwich, England

1935–36

Wireless models AC76 (circular), AD36 (circular)

Client: E. K. Cole Ltd (Ekco)

Architectural Review, December 1935, p. 281

Desk for PEL, 1935

opposite: Wells Coates with a model of Wingsail catamaran, 1946

1936–7

Flexunit Furniture

Client: P. E. Gane, Bristol and B. Burkle and Sons
J. L. Martin and S. Speight, *The Flat Book*, p.94

1936

Grand Piano for Piano Exhibition, Dorland Hall, Lower Regent Street, London

Client: Barratt & Robinson Ltd
Architectural Review, October 1936, p.185
J. L. Martin and S. Speight, *The Flat Book*, p.134

1937

'Thermovent' electric heater (1 or 2kw versions, black or walnut casing)

Client: E. K. Cole Ltd (Ekco)
Art and Industry, February 1938, p. 50
J. L. Martin and S. Speight, *The Flat Book*, p.26–7
Jennifer Hawkins and Marianne Hollis (eds), *Thirties, British Art and Design before the War*, London, Arts Council of Great Britain, 1979, p.232

1939

Blue Mix Dinghy

Client: Wells Coates

1946

Design for 16-ft Wingsail catamaran

Client: Wells Coates
Yachting Monthly, 1946 (model shown at 'Britain Can Make It' exhibition, London, launched 1948)

c. 1946

Wireless model A22 (circular)

Client: E. K. Cole Ltd (Ekco))

1946

Combined Television-Radio set

Client: E. K. Cole Ltd (Ekco)
Michael Farr, *Design in British Industry*, Cambridge, Cambridge University Press, 1955, pl.xxxii & p.77

1947

A33 Radiotime clock-radio set

Client: E. K. Cole Ltd (Ekco)
Royal Society of Arts, Council of Industrial Design, *Design at Work*, London, HMSO, 1948, pp.18–19

1948

P63 Princess portable battery radio

Client: E. K. Cole Ltd (Ekco)
Studio Yearbook of Decorative Art, 1949, p. 124
Michael Farr, *Design in British Industry*, Cambridge, Cambridge University Press, 1955, pp.71–8
Robert Hawes, *Radio Art*, Green Wood, 1991, pp. 46–7, 82, 108
Baker, Malcolm and Richardson, Brenda, eds. *A Grand Design : The Art of the Victoria and Albert Museum*. London: V&A Publications, 1997, p.431

1951

Clocks for Royal Waiting Room, South Bank Exhibition: The King's Clock ('Eight Bells'); The Queen's Clock ('Hour Glass')

Client: Festival of Britain, made by Charles Frodsham & Company
Laura Cohn, *Door to a Secret Room*, p.198

Thermovent heater

Obituary

The early death of Wells Wintemute Coates has deprived modern architecture of one of its pioneers in England. Born in Tokyo in 1895, and educated in Canada, he came to London University as a research student of engineering in 1924. He took his Ph.D. degree there. He was in private practice as an architect in London from 1929-39.

In the formative period of architecture in the early thirties, Wells Coates made a significant contribution. At a time when English architecture has been described as 'broadly Renaissance, inclining to Classic according to the taste of the architect', Wells Coates brought a well-trained mind and natural good taste to bear upon the problems of design and it was then something rare to see an architect paring away the stylistic details and frankly exploiting simplicity. He was keenly interested in the influences which were at work on painting, sculpture and architecture and, with Paul Nash, was one of that little band of early crusaders which formed Unit One. A little later, in 1933, he was largely responsible for the foundation of the MARS (Modern Architectural Research) Group, which was to make its mark upon the younger generation of architects.

In 1930-32, when the British Broadcasting Corporation selected a small group of architects to design and equip contemporary studio interiors for Broadcasting House, I was associated with Wells Coates in this work. He designed the Dramatic Control Room, News Studios and Dramatic Effects and Gramopohone Effects Studios. I regard these as the most significant features of the Broadcasting House experiement.

The equipment and fittings which he designed for these studios still deserve study and were a foretaste of things to come. Such work awakened interest in industrial design and when later, in 1934, he was commissioned to design a moulded plastic radio cabinet for E. K. Cole Ltd., it rapidly became 'the most famous set in British Radio'. Those who do remember it will find it illustrated in Michael Farr's *Design in British Industry* (1955) along with other excellent designs for a portable and a television-radio for the same firm. Later he turned his attention to other types of equipment and eventually, with original results, to the design of small sailing-boats.

His architectural output during the thirties was not great. It included the notable (to some notorious) Lawn Road (or Isokon) Flats – an essay in the economy of space: other flats in Kensington and Brighton; laboratories for Ekco; and shops and houses. It was not an easy period in which to practice modern architecture in England and his work had often a sort of puritan logic about it which did nothing to ingratiate it to the public.

The war interrupted his practice. He had been a fighter-pilot in the First World War. In the second he rose to the rank of Wing Commander and was appointed an OBE. When he resumed his practice his most important work was the Telecinema for the South Bank exhibition of 1951. For some years afterwards his practice was carried on as Wells-Coates, Jacqueline Tyrrwhitt and Associates, and he was chiefly engaged on town planning projects. In 1956 he moved to Vancouver where the promise of his career, on that side of the Atlantic, has now been cut short.

My own recollection of Wells Coates is of his great personal assurance, an assurance which some regarded as conceit. He was good humoured, but also 'touchy' and his friendship was elusive. He was an admirable host. He had great physical vigour and there was a very gay side to his fundamentally serious nature. His conversation was informed and precise, his opinions sincerely expressed. One also remembers his chuckling, happy laugh, but I do not think he enjoyed great personal happiness. Material success seems also to have eluded him, but there can be no doubt that architecture has lost an outstanding personality, as well as a genuine leader.

In an early manifesto for Unit One he wrote: 'The Tradition of Architecture is to seek the order that leads to freedom and fullness of life. Architecture has to serve the purposes of the people as well as the purposes of beauty.' His own work was a search for these principles.

RAYMOND MCGRATH
RIBA Journal, August 1958

Bibliography

Principal Published Writings by Wells Coates

'Criticks: a Reader's Way to Reconcile their Unfriendliness', Letter, *Architects' Journal*, 11 February 1931

'Inspiration from Japan', *Architects' Journal*, 4 November 1931, p.586

'Materials for Architecture', *Architects' Journal*, 4 November 1931, pp.588–9.

'Furniture Today, Furniture Tomorrow – Leaves from a Meta-Technical Notebook', *Architectural Review*, July 1932, pp.29–34.

'Response to Tradition', *Architectural Review*, November 1932, pp.165–8.

'Modern Shops and Modern Materials', *Building*, December 1932, pp.165–8

'Interview with J. Craven Pritchard', *Advertisers' Weekly*, March 1933

'Design in Modern Life-VI. Modern Dwellings for Modern Needs, Boumphrey & Coates', *Listener*, 24 May 1933, pp.819–21

'Wells Coates' in Herbert Read (ed.), *Unit One, the Modern Movement in England, Architecture, Painting and Sculpture*, London, Cassell, 1934, pp.104–15.

'Letter concerning Exhibition of Contemporary Industrial Design in the Home', (co-signatory Serge Chermayeff), *Architects' Journal*, 1 November, 1934, p.641

'Planning in Section', *Architectural Review*, August 1937, pp.51–8.

'The Conditions for an Architecture for To-day', *Architectural Association Journal*, April 1938, pp.447–57.

'Notes on Dwellings for Tomorrow', in Ascot Gas Water Heaters Ltd, *Flats: Municipal & Private Enterprise*, London, Ascot Gas Water Heaters Ltd, 1938, pp.50–5.

'Planning the Festival of Britain Telekinema', *British Kinematography*, 18:4, 1951, pp.108–19.

'The Freedom & Responsibility of the Architect', *Journal of the Royal Architectural Institute of Canada*, May 1952, pp.148–50 and 159.

'Address by Wells Coates to the 1957 Graduation Banquet, UBC', *Journal of the Royal Architectural Institute of Canada*, June 1959, pp.205–11

Principal Archival Sources for Wells Coates

Canadian Centre for Architecture, Montreal, Canada:
Wells Coates Papers

RIBA/V&A Archives, London, England:
Wells Coates Papers
Wells Coates Drawings

University of East Anglia, Norwich, England:
Jack Pritchard Papers

Writing on Wells Coates

Unpublished PhD Theses

Anna Basham, 'From Victorian to Modernist: the changing perception of Japanese Architecture encapsulated in Wells Coates' Japonisme', University of the Arts, 2007

Farouk Elgohary, 'Wells Coates and his position in the Modern Movement in England', University of London, 1965

Books

Sherban Cantacuzino, *Wells Coates, A Monograph*, London, Gordon Fraser, 1978

Laura Cohn (ed.), *Wells Coates, Architect and Designer, 1895–1958*, Oxford, Oxford Polytechnic Press, 1979

The Door to a Secret Room, a Portrait of Wells Coates, Aldershot, Scolar Press, 1999

Articles, Chapters in Books, and Obituaries

Geoffrey Boumphrey, 'The Designers – 6. Wells Coates', *Architectural Review*, January 1936, pp.45–6

The Times, 20 June, 1958, p.13; supplements by Gordon Russell, 25 June 1958, p.13 and Patrick Heron, 16 July 1958, p.14

Builder, 27 June, 1958, p.1178

Journal of the Royal Institute of Architects of Canada, June 1959, p.216

Raymond McGrath, 'Mr Wells Wintemute Coates,' *RIBA Journal*, August 1958, p.357

J. M. Richards, 'Wells Coates 1893–1958', *Architectural Review*, December 1958, pp.357–60

Randal Bell, 'The Client Looks Back: Mechanism of Design', *Architectural Review*, November 1979, pp.312–3

Elspeth Cowell, 'Wells Coates' Toronto Island Redevelopment Project', *Bulletin for the Society for the Study of Architecture in Canada*, vol.20, no.2, pp. 41–50

Elizabeth Darling, 'Wells Coates: maker of modern British architecture' *Architectural Review*, September 2008, pp.82–7

— '...[T]he scene in which the daily drama of personal life takes place': towards the modern interior in early 1930s Britain', in B. Martin et al. (eds), *Designing the Modern Interior, from the Victorians to Today*, Oxford, Berg, 2009, pp.95–105.

Berthold Lubetkin, 'The disillusioned looks back' [letter to Wells Coates, 10 January 1933, and corollary, 31 July 1979], *Architectural Review*, November 1979, p. 330

General writings on British Modernism, with special relevance to Coates

Cheryl Buckley, *Designing Modern Britain*, London, Reaktion, 2007

Michael Collins, (ed.), *Hampstead in the Thirties: a committed decade*, London, Camden Arts Centre, 1974

Elizabeth Darling, *Re-forming Britain, Narratives of Modernity before Reconstruction*, London, Routledge, 2007

David Dean, *The Thirties, Recalling the Architectural Scene*, London, Trefoil Books, 1983

John Gold, *The Experience of Modernism, Modern Architects and the Future City, 1928–53*, London, E & FN Spon, 1997

Alistair Grieve, *Isokon for ease, for ever*, London, Isokon Plus Ltd., 2004

Jennifer Hawkins and Marianne Hollis (eds), *Thirties, British Art and Design before the War*, London, Arts Council of Great Britain, 1979

Anthony Jackson, *The Politics of Architecture: a History of Modern Architecture in Britain*, London, Architectural Press, 1970.

Duncan Miller, *Interior Decorating*, London, The Studio Ltd, 1937.

The Museum of Modern Art, *Modern Architecture in England*, Museum of Modern Art, New York, 1937

Alan Powers, *Britain, Modern Architectures in History*, London, Reaktion, 2007

Jack Pritchard, *View from a Long Chair, the Memoirs of Jack Pritchard*, London, Routledge & Kegan Paul, 1984

John Summerson, 'Introduction' in Trevor Dannatt (ed), *Modern Architecture in Britain*, London, B.T.Batsford Ltd, 1959, pp. 11–28

Rhodri Windsor Liscombe, *The New Spirit. Modern Architecture in Vancouver, 1938–1963*, Montreal, Canadian Centre for Architecture, 1997

F. R. S. Yorke and Frederick Gibberd, *The Modern Flat*, London, The Architectural Press, 1937

Index

Note: page numbers in italics refer to illustrations.

Picture Credits

Anon.: 35, 36, 104, 148 (bottom)
Architects' Journal (courtesy of RIBA library): 27 (top), 51 (all), 54 (both), 81 (all), 110, 115, 144 (both), 145 (top), 149 (bottom right), 150, 151, 153 (top)
Architectural Design and Construction: 149 (bottom left)
Architectural Review: 14 (top), 29 (both), 45, 46, 68 (top), 70–71, 85 (both), 86, 91 (courtesy of Gordon Cullen Estate), 102–103, 105, 145 (bottom), 147 (bottom), 149 (top)
Estate of John Armstrong, courtesy of Paul Liss: 124 (bottom)
Avanti Architects: ii, 132, 133 (both), 134
Canadian Centre for Architecture, Montreal: 78 (bottom), 79, 80, 94, 100, 101, 114, 118, 124 (top)
Canadian Centre for Architecture, Montreal / Laura Cohn: 4, 10, 12 (both), 14 (bottom), 15 (both), 19, 43 (bottom), 44, 55, 78 (top), 92, 93 (both)
Wells Coates: 43 (top)
Laura Cohn: 18 (both), 24 (both), 28 (both), 30 (both), 31 (both), 32 (both), 33, 40 (both), 41, 47 (both), 75 (both), 90, 95, 116, 117 (top), 123, 146, 148 (top), 152
James O. Davies, English Heritage: front cover, x, 52–53, 56 (both), 82, 88 (both), 89, 130
Design Council / University of Brighton Archives www.brighton.ac.uk/designarchives: back cover, 98 (top), 112, 122
gta Archives, ETH Zurich: CIAM archives: 107 (both)
The Estate of Patrick Heron. All rights reserved, DACS 2012: 9 (right)
James Gray Collection, the photographic archive of the Regency Society of Brighton and Hove, www.regencysociety-jamesgray.com: 74
Penlee House Gallery & Museum, Penzance: 23
Photo: Nicholas Kane; courtesy of Avanti Architects: 69
Kensington Central Library: 27 (bottom)
Martin and Speight, *The Flat Book*, London, Heinemann, 1939: 153 (bottom), 154 (both)
Millar & Harris, courtesy of the British Library: 37, 38 (both), 39 (both)
National Monuments Record / English Heritage: 67, 120 (bottom)
National Portrait Gallery, London: xii, 48
By kind permission of Tronn Overend: 16–17
John Piper / Laura Cohn: 84
Pritchard Papers, University of East Anglia: 50 (both), 66, 68 (bottom), 128
RIBA Library Drawings & Archives Collections: 57, 58, 62, 64 (both), 109, 117 (bottom), 120 (top), 126, 142
Science & Society Picture Library, Science Museum: 97 (top)
Courtesy of Southend Museum: 97 (bottom left and bottom right), 98 (bottom left and bottom right)
Dorothea St John George: 9 (left)
Morley von Sternberg, courtesy of Paul Zara: vi, 76–77, 136, 139 (both), 140
Studio Yearbook of Decorative Art: 147 (top)
Edith Tudor-Hart: 60
Courtesy of Paul Zara: 137 (both)